MW01485046

THE USHERS, PROTOCOLS AND GREETERS THAT EVERY CHURCH NEEDS

BY

ALBERT O. AINA

Albert O. Aina

CHRISTIAN LEADERSHIP SKILLS INC.

P. O. Box 51250, Falomo - Ikoyi, Lagos - Nigeria

Tel.: +234 (0) 8023010696, 08023228828

email: albertoaina@yahoo.com

www.christianleadershipskills.org

CONTENTS

The Mandate

The same thing you are giving to the business world, package it, give it to my church, beginning from the Bible.

Empower the business people

Raise for Me quality leaders

Give youths a sense of purpose and achievement.

ALBERT O. AINA

Since September, 1994

Introduction

WHY I FINALLY WROTE THIS BOOK 20 YEARS LATER

I started writing this book in 1994. That was the year the LORD graciously commissioned me to raise for Him Quality leaders. I started with Ministers' and Pastors' workshop. Training for ushers was the second assignment I handled among the three fold mandates the LORD gave me in 1994. But, no book was written by me back then, neither did I come across any specialized book on Ushers, Greeters and Protocols in one volume, 20 years ago.

I have been privileged to conduct Training courses across the length and breadth of Nigeria on Ushering ministry for 20 years. I have interacted with over 400 churches from over 280 denominations in conferences and seminars but I never wrote a book on this topic. Our outfit, Christian Leadership Skills, have been involved in mass training for ushers in churches that counted 120,000 on Sundays with Ushers' workforce of about 4,000. I have written 36 books todate, but none on Ushers, Protocol and Greeters until now.

A particular mega church invited us to deliver training

for ushers and crowd controllers twice within three months in their headquarters church. Their invitation came a bit late I could not be there physically. I didn't have a book on Ushers or crowd control. Only a manual.

Churches get confused on the role of ushers as different from protocol officers. I have witnessed ushers and protocols fight for territories in churches. A particular church head usher insists that he must stay side by side with the protocol officer by the altar, very close to the anointed. There was no book to show where each belong.

A particular ministry scrapped the word "Ushers" from the list of ministries. The General Overseer banned the entire ushers from officiating in the length and breadth of the church. His reason? Brethren have the Holy Spirit to direct them. No need for Ushers and the church went on "smoothly thereafter". I had no book to give to the man of God. No book I could give, until 20 years later!

Who are Ushers? Who are Protocol officers? Who are Greeters? Who are Traffic Controllers? I didn't write any book to explain. I only explain during workshop session. Now the explanation has become handy.

THE USHERS, PROTOCOLS AND GREETERS THAT EVERY CHURCH NEEDS is twenty years old in writing. But the facts are over 4,000 years old. 1 found vivid description of eight categories of Ushers, Protocols and Greeters ministry in first and second Chronicles.

Queen of Sheba remarked on King Solomon's PAS', Protocol officers and aid-de camp in II Chron. 9:7.

Surveillance officers and Security Ushers were fully operational in Solomon era in Song of Solomon 3:3. It took me twenty years to bring 4,000 years of ancient practices into today's Facebook congregation.

I have taught Customer Relations in corporate setting. I have instructed Personal Assistants, Company Secretaries in high profile client management. I have lectured on Public Relations in established government institutions as a management consultant for over twenty years. When God called me in1994 "to take the same thing you are giving the business world, package it and give it to My church, beginning from the Bible", I understood the mandate of my calling.

An Usher slapped a newcomer in a regional church during worship service. His reason? The newcomer refused the seat he was offered. Ushers, Protocols and Greeters are in leadership roles essentially. Churches don't see them as such. Church leaders often see them as beginning or stating points of ministry. You will discover these categories of church workers as the face of the church. Ushers, Protocols and Greeters represent both who and what the church is to anyone passing through its doors. This category of ministers hold a vital key to the growth or non-growth of your church. Ushers, Protocols and Greeters hold a vital key to lock the back door of the church or open it wide. See what I mean in the first chapter.

That is why you will see the ushers, Greeters and Protocol ministry in a different light in the following pages. You will then understand why it has taken me twenty years to write this book.

I still run the courses. I run the workshop for Ushers, Protocols and Greeters as God enables.

Call me on 08023010696

Email me albertoaina@yahoo.com

The Worshiper Who Never Comes Back

I am a nice worshiper you all knew me. I am the one who never complains, no matter what kind of service I get.

I entered into the church premises, no one notices me. The Usher hurriedly passed me into church service as if I was disturbing the traffic. When I tried to pack my car on my first visit to the church he yelled and barked at me because I was wrongly parked. I did not complain. I even greeted him heartily, but I was answered under breath with scant murmur. I took it.

I entered with my heavily pregnant wife who desired to stay in the airy part of the auditorium and close to "Ladies", but we were snubbed and treated as troublesome by protocol officers on duty.

The day's bulletin was pressed into our hands, as if we were beggars. I tried to compliment the Usher for his kindness, he won't bother to look at my face.

I took up the hymn book during congregational song, it

was snatched from me by the usher, saying I ought to share with others. I never complained, even though I would have happily shared this if I was told.

As we stood to go after service, we were ordered to move out "without making noise". I didn't nag. Not even one person standing as usher or protocol ever smiled or looked at our "sinful faces" all though the solemn service.

I came following Sunday hoping for a better reception this time, I got none. Still I never complained; that is uncalled for. No, I am the nice worshiper. And I'll tell you who else I am. I'm the worshiper who never comes back!

Section A

BIBLICAL FOUNDATION FOR USHERING,

PROTOCOLS AND GREETERS MINISTRY

Chapter 1: Is My Ministry Mentioned In The Bible

Ushering, Protocols and Greeters belong to the ministry of help. *"And God hath set some in the church, first Apostles, secondarily Prophets thirdly Teachers, after that Miracles, then gifts of healing, helps, governments diversities of tongues"* (1 Cor. 12:28).

In the Greek, helps is ANTILEPSIS, meaning a support, help, succourer, an aid. They are in the same class as Deacons and Deaconesses. Literal meaning of their duties is "one who gives assistance and support." The scriptures reveal several important truths.

1. The Ushering, Protocols and Greeters ministry is ordained and anointed by God Himself. Ushers, protocols and Greeters have been divinely set in the church for a purpose.

2. Ushers, Protocols and Greeters are as important as other offices and ministries as Apostles, Teachers and Leadership.

3. They are supernatural ministries like miracles and healing.

Chapter 2: Six Reasons Why Ushers, Protocols And Greeters Are Vital To Any Church

A pastor was asked to choose just one worker to follow him to start a new church in a new location, among the following: Sunday School teacher, Choir, Intercessor, Song Leader, Assistant Pastor, Usher, Building Committee, Children Worker.

He looked well and decided to pick an usher. Why? He said the Usher would be there to arrange the place and settle the people for him, while preaching. He needed someone to let people be orderly so they can listen to what he was preaching. Usher would let him know how he is doing from his record and observation.

Ushering, protocols and greeters ministry are most vital, if not to everyone, but to the pastor and the members.

Six reasons why are the ushers, protocols, and greeters so vital.

1. They are the best companion/helper to the pastor.

2. They create the first impression – they are the first contact with all worshippers, particularly the first timers. They are receptionists/public relation officers.

3. They guarantee security in the place of worship. They

determine who enters. They observe all inside and lock the door. They give people peace of mind.

4. They handle the job that no one can handle, especially the most difficult, dirty and undignified work. They stand throughout, no matter how long the service. They clean and dust the chairs, sweep the place of worship, flush the toilets, carry/attend to crying babies. They hardly concentrate as other members of the church on the sermon, but on the people. They expose themselves to dangers of robbers, assassins, witches and area boys.

5. They are the first to come and last to go.

6. They keep the leadership informed of progress, or otherwise, through attendance/spiritual report.

Chapter 3: Forty Desirable Characteristic Traits Of Ushers, Protocols And Greeters

WHAT IS CHARACTER?

According to Webster's dictionary, character is the aggregate of distinctive qualities, qualities that stand out and have a positive net effect.

There are a listing of about 247 character traits on the internet. Ushers, Protocol and Greeters ministries are essentially leadership roles within the context of the church. As a matter of fact, they are in the same class as Deacons and Deaconesses. Apart from the Pastoral ministry.

Ushers, Greeters and Protocols are the face of the church. They represent both who and what your church is to anyone walking through its doors of the 247 desirable character traits listed on the internet, the following 40 traits are selected as being most crucial in the discharge of the ministry of Ushers, Protocols and Greeters.

FORTY (40) CHARACTER TRAITS MOST DESIRABLE

1.   Attentive

2. Amiable

3. Active

4. Affordable

5. Conscious

6. Considerate

7. Cheerful

8. Dutiful

9. Enthusiastic

10. Friendly

11. Happy

12. Helpful

13. Faithful

14. Jovial

15. Kind

16. Loving

17. Confident

18. Mature

19. Cooperative

20. Obedient

21. Persistent

22. Peaceful

23. Respectful

24. Responsive

25. Responsible

26. Sincere

27. Sensitive

28. Hospitable

29. Thorough

30. Tactful

31. Proactive

32. Useful

33. Wise

34. Warm hearted

35. Polite

36. Dependable

37. Smart

38. Loyal

39. Disciplined

40. Tolerant

Section B
SPECIALIZED CATEGORIES WITHIN

USHERS, PROTOCOLS AND GREETERS

MINISTRY

Chapter 4: Eight Specialized Categories Within Ushers, Protocol And Greeters Ministry

There are eight categories of ushers, protocols and greeters, each with distinctive job demands and specifications. These are vital for proper on-the-job training. They all belong to the ministry of helps and have the following specialities.

1. THE GREETERS:

They welcome people into the auditorium. They spend most of their time outside the church auditorium. Greeters must wear permanent smiles and have open arms to shake hands and embrace worshippers as appropriate. They welcome everyone to the church with prophetic/uplifting words. It is good to hear the following from greeters: "You are lifted," "Today is your day," "You are highly favoured" etc. The greeters should comprise both male and female. Their dress code is different from usual ushers. Their clothes should be corporate and reflective of the congregation. *"And the porters waited at every gate; they might not depart from their service, for their brethren the Levites prepared for them."* (II Chro. 35: 15b). It is expected that this department have big umbrellas handy during raining season or hot season to provide shade for worshippers from the gate to the church auditorium. Greeters' seats are usually marked and reserved for them when they come inside the auditorium. Their work continues inside the auditorium. They are to watch out for newcomers that respond to altar call or greetings from the Pastor. If they are many, greeters should assist and escort older members, officials and invited guests to their seats.

2. SANCTUARY USHERS:

These are conventional ushers that are posted within the church to welcome, guide and direct people to their seats. They should know how many people a seat can accommodate. They give attention to the needs of worshipers and to keep people awake, especially when the message is going on. *"Among these were the division of the porters, even among the chief men, having wards one against another, to minister in the House of the Lord"* (1 Chro. 26:12). It is recommended that one sanctuary usher should maintain ten rows. They are to ensure that worshippers fill the seat from the front to the back. Sanctuary ushers see to the collection of offerings and provide envelopes.

3. ROVING/PATROL USHERS (ALSO

CALLED SECURITY USHERS OR SURVEILLANCE OFFICERS):

Their duty is to go up and down to see to the welfare and security of the congregation. They provide link between outside ushers and inside ushers. They take information from the car park ushers to those in the sanctuary. Their ministry reduces the need for ushers to move up and down and away from their duty posts. They are to regularly check the back of the auditorium, and especially areas that are not often used in the church. They check offices, while service is going on and challenge any loitering and wandering. ***"The watch that go about the city found me."*** (Songs of Solomon 3:3). They need to be provided with walkie talkies, GSM or radio facilities.

4. ALTAR USHERS:

They serve as Aide-De-Camp to Pastors, Officiating Ministers and Choirs. Not every usher can serve at the altar. Experience is vital. High level of alertness and extra sensitivity are needed to serve at the altar. It is not for junior ranks. It is best to post able bodied and spirit filled men to this position as they serve more as personal guards, the type that stand behind VIP's in public gatherings.

We have had cases of evil minded persons coming to the altar to assault or even wound officiating ministers. *"Happy are thy men and happy are these thy servants, which stand continually before thee and hear thy wisdom."* (II Chron 9:7). Their work continues even after the ministers have left the altar. They provide a shield to them on their way to their offices or vehicles, to avoid mob action or disturbance. They stand behind the pastor's door for, at least one hour, after service to see to their needs and attend and screen those who need Pastor's attention, after service.

5. SPECIAL DUTY USHERS:

This category serves as under cover plain cloth, security, detective, intelligence agents. They don't wear identity tags. Their assignment is to identify unfamiliar faces, and monitor suspicious movements. In churches where visitors are usually invited to the front row, it is advisable to allow two or more special duty ushers to go and sit in their midst so as to eavesdrop on any conversation that may be found useful in preventing evil. Some of them can be assigned to either drive a guest speaker or serve as aide-de-camp to them in the course of their stay. They confirm hotel bookings, clear their luggage's, and confirm ticketing and boarding passes at airport. Serving or retired military and service men will do well in this department.

6. PROTOCOL OFFICERS (Pastor's Aides):

Their duty is essentially personal. It is to make guests comfortable, especially when many important dignitaries are being expected for special programmes. They escort dignitaries from their cars to their seats and back to their vehicles. They work with Altar ushers and greeters regularly. They provide refreshment for guests before, during and after each programme. Where gallands and flowers and tokens are to be presented to guests, protocols provide the lead.

7. CROWD CONTROLLERS/ENFORCERS:

The services of crowd controllers become useful in a very large congregation and in camps, convention and crusade grounds. Their work is to resist unruly persons. They are to prevent nuisance and urchins from entering the church, and caution people who are unruly and, in rare occasions, apply minimum force to ensure order or prevent crime. They work with uniformed security personnel, where available, to provide undercover detective security. They need walkie - talkie to facilitate their work.

8. CAR PARK USHERS:

This class of ushers ensure the orderliness, convenience and security of worshippers' vehicles within the Church premises. Their most important service is to give worshippers peace of mind all through the service as to the security of their cars. These ushers must arrive their duty posts at least 30 minutes to all regular services. It is an advantage if licensed drivers are among the team to provide necessary assistance to elderly seniors, learners or even ladies in parking their cars. They are to provide car pass to every worshippers before parking their cars. They record every car in attendance. They are to take notice of additional new cars and notice which member brings a new car they also notice any malfunction in the vehicles and observe when a worshipper fail to bring his/her car. They are to be weary of visitors to the car park asking for owners of parked vehicles. Red flags should be handy as well as reflective traffic uniforms provided for car park ushers. Cars with head lamp on or flat tyres should be discretely notified to the owners in the course of the service.

Chapter 5: Job Descriptions OF An Usher

"And the LORD took the man and put him in the Garden of Eden to tend and guard and keep it" (Gen 2: 15 - Amplified)

In the above text is to be found a concise description of what the ushers work entails in the context of the church. The work of an Usher consists of:

a. TENDING,

b. GUARDING and

c. KEEPING.

Oxford Advanced Learners Dictionary list the functions of an Usher to include: Showing people to their seats, doorkeeper in law court.

THREE TENDING DUTIES OF USHERS

To tend is to watch-over, attend to, serve customers.

a. **Watching over:** as assistants to the Pastor's Ministry. Looking over the congregation - physically, spiritually (Prov. 27:23).

b. **Attend to:** give care and thought, listen carefully, pay attention to, wait on, look after.

c. **Serve Customers:** who are the customers? This entails supplying need, as servants and companion, to be polite, kind, courteous.

FOUR ASPECTS OF BEING A GUARD

This entails four aspects

a. Being in the state of watchfulness against attack, dangers, or surprises like a sentry or soldier (Neh. 4:21-23; I Peter 5:8).

b. Attitude of readiness to defend oneself or others

against an attack or surprises like a boxer (Neh. 4:9; Luke 27:47-51; II Cor. 10:4-6).

c. Body of soldiers with the duty of protecting, honouring or escorting a person - Pastor, Guest speaker, New comers (Acts 23:23-24).

d. Using care and caution to prevent danger. *"Be well balanced - temperate, sober minded, be vigilant and cautious at all times, for that enemy of yours, the devil roam around like a lion roaring (in fierce anger), seeking someone to seize upon and devour."* (I Peter 5:8). This includes putting ear to the ground for gossips, nose in the air, eye wide open, especially during prayers (except otherwise instructed) for pick pockets, bible stealers, purse thieves during prayers and offering and altar calls. Check on women sitting postures directly in front of the altar.

THE EIGHT KEEPING DUTIES OF USHERS

a. To cause something or somebody to remain in a specified state or position - children, sleeping saints, wanderers careless movement, etc.

b. Watch over closely, keep an eye (John 10: 10)

c. Remember something (keep in mind). It is ability to accurately observe and describe person - square face, long face, broad face, long head, high crown head, flat in the back places, etc (Mark 14:66-70)

d. Keep A tab on: Military intelligence. I Sam. 26:4 Suspicious movement, stage actions or look, especially new persons, outsiders, worshippers, a member from congregation with a note, etc.

e. Prevent, hold back, refrain from doing something injurious to the church

f. Pay proper respect to or be faithful to appointments.

g. Keep records, count number, make notes of preachers and spiritual records.

h. Be responsible for the house-keeping work: cleaning, sweeping and arranging.

TWELVE (12) CORE DUTIES OF USHERS IN A CHURCH

1. Spiritual Intelligence, Military Alertness, Tactfulness,

Smart, Personal discipline, Combat readiness at all times - spiritual and physical as Safety and security officer.

2. The first to get to Church and the last to live

3. Cleanliness of the venue and readiness for service.

4. Prayer intercessors - Is. 62:6-7.

5. Receptionists to welcome and receive worshipers.

6. Seating Arrangement: Must know the seating capacity of the auditorium. How many bench per row, how many can sit on a bench/row. In cases of fat people, to make adjustments.

7. Security Intelligent Officers - mark any suspicious, object, person and inform head ushers. Look around flower pots, window/doors, see if any was opened before you came in, offering box broken? Check.

8. Take note and take care of new comers, disabled and children.

9. Spiritual discipline during service - when to allow people in, when to stop prophecy - taking instruction from altar/ head ushers.

10. Offering collection with honesty - Neh. 7: 1-3

11. Keeping secret. Not talkative.

12. He should realize he is under authority, Obey before complain - II Cor. 10:6.

Chapter 6: Protocol Officers (The Pastor's Aide)

WHAT IS PROTOCOL?

The word protocol is another word for divine order.

PURPOSE AND EXPECTATION OF A PASTOR'S AIDE (PROTOCOL OFFICER)

The main duty of a protocol officer is to ensure the comfort and security of the pastorates and members of the congregation.

In addition, they are to ensure the smooth running of services and programs organized by the church.

In summary, the protocol officer is the eyes, the legs and ears of the pastorate.

FIFTEEN QUALITIES OF AN EFFECTIVE PROTOCOL

1. He/she must be agile. .

2. He/she must be very intelligent.

3. He/she must be a good manager, exercising excellent initiative with less supervision.

4. Smart in out-look and dressing- he/she must sustain a good clean appearance.

5. His/her shoe must be clean and shinned at all times.

6. His/her hair must be well groomed, nails done (No dirty nails, well manicured).

7. Perfumed/body spray

8. Suit well laundered.

9. Handkerchiefs (Always carry one. It comes very handy).

10. Mouth clean and well flossed.

11. Spiritually sensitive.

12. Good and effective communication skill.

13. Good natural psychology.

14. Knowing the pastor's likes and dislikes.

15. Know when to talk and when to be talked to.

TWELVE (12) DUTIES OF' PROTOCOL OFFICERS

1. Anticipate and prepare for the arrival of ministers and expected guests by:

   a. Allotting arranging special/separate car parks

   b. Creating separate entrance/exit for the special guests to protect them against being shuffled by the crowd.

2) They should be in the know as to the timing and order of arrival for VIP's at the events venue.

3) They escort Ministers and expected guests from their cars to their seats. Where gallands, tokens and flowers are to be provided, protocols show the way.

4) They are to see to the proper sitting position and protocol arrangement at the altar or podium.

5) They are to liaise with personal aids to the VIP's on how best to assist them throughout the event.

6) To monitor and screen all appointments, messages or notes to VIP, Speakers, once seated.

7) To be involved in the choice and arrangement and speed of vehicle to be used. If a convoy movement will be necessary. (Escort arrangements, Communication, Security etc.)

8) To ensure that the order of the conduct of the event is moving with chronological precision

9) To mount wall of protection around VIPs, Speakers and Guests to avoid stampede or mob action.

10. Keep eagles eyes on people at the event to prevent a breach of security (e.g. Terrorist, Hoodlums, Area Boys, Thieves etc.)

11. Be prompt to identify and remove any person that constitutes potential distractions (e.g. Antagonist, Spiritually oppressed, mentally and Physically ill and Street Urchin, etc.)

12. To plan for orderly and timely departure of VIPs and ease of movement at the each day's programme, particularly at night.

Chapter 7: Ten Ways To Treat Guest Ministers Couteously

1. Accord all guests, either main speakers or not, deserve the same type of treatment and attention.

2. Familiarize yourself with the guest names as well his/her Church's names and location.

3. Use Sir/Ma for your conversations.

4. Know their preference for drinks, food, personal and special needs before hand.

5. Find out how many people or aides are coming with him before hand.

6. Make sure the lodging and accommodation meets their taste.

7. Take time to check out the accommodation and

conveniences before time

8. Learn to stay clear, but near, when Pastor is having chit chat with the guests.

9. No external interference should hinder you from doing your job and keeping your standard, not even the guest's PA. The guest's PA can be at the background because his attention may be needed.

10. Be able to anticipate what next, always have a pen, and handkerchief ready.

Chapter 8: Twelve Duties Of Greeters, Host And Hostess Ministries

1. To welcome and greet all worshippers to the service beginning from the gate.

2. To conscientiously assist the worshippers, especially the new comer, in seating in the appropriate seat during the service.

3. To help every worshipper with personal effects and placing their children in the children church.

4. To seat, only when their allocated rows are full, and to anticipate the needs of the worshippers in their allocated section/row of the church. e.g. need to go to toilets, information e.tc.

5. To identity new comers in the church and to specially greet and present the welcome pack to new worshipper during pastoral welcome during the

service.

6. To usher the new comers to the conference room/reception center and extend hospitality to them i.e. refreshment, introduction, etc.

7. The host or greeter is to be constantly aware of the power of "first time favourable impression'.

8. While in the conference room, the head of department or his/her representative shall brief the new comers on:

   (a) The full name of the church and what the church stands for.

   (b) The leadership of the church i.e. the Senior Pastor, assisting ministers, their spouses and their backgrounds.

   (c) The relevant ministries in the church as they apply to the new comers. A married woman will be interested in the women ministry, single lady will like to know about youth programmes and ladies ministries.

(d) Worship schedules on Sundays, Tuesday, Wednesday, Thursday, especially the oncoming ones for that particular week.

(e) How Sunday school and home fellowship cell centers will help the new comer

(f) Recall two to three powerful testimonies in the church.

(g) Ask if he/she has any questions or prayer requests.

9. The host/hostess/greeter is to assist the new comer to fill the visitor's card.

10. The Head of Department (HOD) is to compile this list in the department register, forward copies to the Head of Ministry (HOM) of visitation/follow-up department.

11. It is expected that the HOD will inform the head usher about the numbers of new comers every Sunday.

12. The HOD is to submit a report along with comment to the Senior Pastor at the end of the month, through the head of ministry operations.

Chapter 9: Eighteen Roles And Duties Of a Surveillance Officer

1. Ensure there is no theft in the service e.g. phones, bags etc.

2. Ensure effective and proper functioning of gadgets e.g. Microphones, projectors etc.

3. Ensure the comfort of the members during the service e.g. put on fans, air conditioners, etc.

4. Ensure free flow of movement of people before, during and after the service

5. Coordinate the other sub unit i.e. ensure the information / directives are properly carried out

6. Ensure the safety of the offering baskets

7. Must be Born Again and Holy Spirit filled

8. He must be proactive

9. He must be able to communicate effectively. Pass his idea and thoughts across clearly

11. He must be able to use the communication gadgets effectively

12. He/She must be able to move strategically in the crowd without causing distraction

13. He/she must be physically fit

14. He must be able to understand radio codes and languages.

15. Humility: An individual who never says "it is not my job". But who is willing to do whatever needs to be done to get the job done

16. Organizational skills; ability to remember minute details for any possible contingency

17. Cooperation: able to deal with any personality

18. Selfless: must not be over ambitious or conscious of personal reward.

Chapter 10: Effective Gate Surveillance And Traffic Control

If a pedestrian can carry out stolen property, a vehicle can remove a thousand times as much. This is why effective Gate Control of Vehicles is so important. This is why it must cover not only outside carriers, but the Church's own transport, visitors' and employees' cars, contractors' vehicles and service vans.

1. Be sure you know the various Passes that your church uses, and to which vehicles they apply.

2. All vehicles entering must be provided with an appropriate Pass, unless they already hold some form of semi-permanent pass issued by the Church.

3. Where outside car parks for employees and visitors are provided, their vehicles should not be allowed in without special authorization.

4. Where inside car parks are provided for employees, their vehicles must display the appropriate Pass. This

is in addition to the drivers and passengers carrying personal identity cards.

5. Where goods vehicles carry a 'mate', or when several visitors occupy one car, each person should be issued with a separate Pass.

6. Make sure that goods vehicles present the correct documentation. If not, check with Delivery or Despatch before issuing a Vehicle Pass.

7. Check with a Visitor's host before issuing a Pass or Passes.

8. Ensure that every Goods vehicle, Contractor's vehicle and service vehicle is properly logged, and that Visitors fill in the Visitors Book correctly and sign it.

Remember that if time is spent to ensure proper procedures are followed for all vehicles, drivers and passengers entering, you will save a lot of time and trouble when they leave.

You are an officer of the Church - your appearance and

manner reflects upon the Church's image. Make sure you display courtesy, fact and efficiency. That is the best way to win respect and detect criminal acts.

You are probably the first Church official that visitors, worshippers and outsiders will come across. So it is up to you to create a good impression. Six cardinal rules to observe at all times.

1. Be smart in your appearance

2. Be confident in yourself.

3. Be sure of your duties and responsibilities.

4. Be firm but fair with all persons you have to question or instruct.

5. Be pleasant, but not over-friendly in your manner.

6. Be sure never to show favouritism or prejudice in your actions.

TEN DUTIES OF PARKING LOT AND SECURITY

PERSONNEL

1. Be at your duty post 30 minutes before all regular services, or as directed by your team leader

2. Park the vehicles in an orderly fashion, each row and each space to be filled in order to maximize the total facility

3. Cars should be parked in the same direction, filling the closest spaces first and in order

4. Park buses and over sized vehicles out of the way, then unload near the door and park them out of the parking traffic patterns

5. Some of the team with driver's license should be assigned to help the elderly seniors, or ladies to park their cars

6. Some workers should be assigned to help Pastors, and escort the elderly from their car to the building.

7. Use all available space

8. Keep prayer watch over the vehicles and the owners

9. Beware of visitors at the park asking to see the owner of certain vehicles

10. Use tact

Chapter 11: Ushering At Crusades, Weddings, Funerals And Special Services

Ushers may be called into ministry at time and situations other than the Sunday worship services.

CRUSADE USHERS

A series of revival services, crusade or retreat may last from a couple of evenings to entire week. Various speakers may be invited at such occasions. Sometimes special musicians are invited to share their testimonies and minister in songs. In such meetings the programme may run throughout the whole day divided into three sessions - morning, afternoon and evening sessions. At each session, the ushers cannot afford to be absent from the meeting due to their special peculiar duties and assignment which is, welcoming and ensuring comfort and safety.

At such special meetings what does the team of usher do? Firstly, the ushers perform all these ministries that they perform at regular services with emphasies on welcoming and ensuring comfort and safety. Secondly, the ushers should arrive well before the service, revival or crusade begins. This is specially true if guest musicians are invited to take part in the service. The team of ushers should know in advance so that they can prepare the space where they will stay and minister.

Some ushers may be detailed to be with the guest musicians. Such ushers will brief the guest artist where the toilets and other conveniencies are located within the premises. Sometimes the musicians may need assistance with their equipment. A good usher will offer to assist in carrying equipment and will offer to help with the set up, but only if asked. An usher should never take it upon him or herself to try to assemble the music equipment without being invited to do so by the musician. Thirdly, the team of ushers should remain after such services has ended to tidy up the place of meeting.

USHERS AT WEDDINGS

The usher's tasks here is to help the wedding party be aware of and locate items they might need for the wedding. Where are the restroom and drinking fountain? Where can bridal party leave things securely? Where is the couple kneeler? etc. At such occasion, the usher must not be far from the presiding minister.

At such occasion, usher must arrive early for the wedding to ensure the doors are open, lights put on, all windows and fans put in order. Guests to the wedding may need the services of ushers, such requests be met humbly lest the church be given a bad image by the unruly behaviour of an usher. Remember these guests who come for wedding are not all members of the host church and may not come back to that church again. Therefore, treat them with honour and respect. Sometimes, the same church hall is used for reception. The ushers should remain after the reception is completed to put the church hall in order and make sure everything is put in proper place in readiness for the next day service and after that, take time to pray and give thanks to God for a successful wedding.

USHERS AT FUNERALS

All the things that we said above about the ushers at weddings also apply to ushers at funerals with the following exceptions.

* The pastor and the funeral director will be in-charge. The family of the deceased may choose ushers among close friends, or the family may ask the pall bearers to serve as ushers. The regular ushering team is there to assist and to provide needed supplies and equipment.

* The ushers and the funeral director need to agree on where the family might wait before entering the sanctuary. In some cases, the family arrives last and the seating of the family marks the beginning of the funeral service. If this is the case, the family may choose to arrive at the church several minutes earlier and wait in a convenient room before being seated in the sanctuary. If this is the case, a room must be provided by the usher, with comfortable chair, fans etc.

* In a case where the family of the deceased arranged for their own special usher, the regular team of ushers of the church have no duties during the service unless emergency situation arises.

* However, lingering after the service to tidy up the sanctuary for the next service is necessary.

Chapter 12: Crows Control And Management

The crowd in this case includes:

a. Spectators, conference participants

b. Guest speakers

c. The special guests and VIPs

d. Denominational Officials

e. Structure and Facilities

CROWD COMPOSITION AND CONTROL

We should expect mixed multitude comprising members of your church, other denominations, non-Christians, commercial vendors and area boys/thieves.

1. There must be proper scrutiny at the entrance gates. Special attention to be focused on hoodlums who should be prevented from coming in.

2. Movement of congregation and conventioners to be strictly monitored with close surveillance.

3. Activities of conventioneers should be especially monitored when popular guest speakers are on the programme

4. Plan for ease of movement at the end of each day's programme, particularly at night. Throughfare and street light should be put in place for up to 500 metres from the convention ground.

GUEST SPEAKERS

1. Escorts must be provided for Guest speakers from the car to the podium and back to their cars.

2. Head usher must be in the arrangement to have knowledge as to security of the hotels where they are lodged.

3. All appointments with the Speakers should be

monitored and must pass through the Altar ushers on duty and the chairman for the session / daily programme.

4. Their cars to be parked at the VIP reserved park.

VIP, GUESTS AND OFFICIALS

1. A separate entrance and exit should be created for them to protect them against being shuffled by the crowd

2. They must have separate car parking space allotted to them.

3. Ushers' wall of protection should be mounted around the VIPs.

4. VIP and officials should have identifying badges.

STRUCTURE / FACILITIES

Ushers should be placed on guard in the following arrears:

1. Computer and Registration Room

2. Generators and Transformer installation

3. Adequate light should be provided around the convention ground to prevent evil doers from hatching their plans.

4. Car parks

5. Areas that are less used.

Section C

YOUR USHERS AND PROTOCOLS EITHER CLOSE YOUR CHURCH'S BACKDOOR OR LEAVE IT WIDE OPEN

Chapter 13: Why Worshippers Come To Church

In "Christianity Today", Dr. Win Ann tells of a survey he carried out with 10,000 people to determine how they became Christians and members in their respective churches. The results were as follows

3 - 5% simply walked into the church and stayed

4 - 6% came because of the Pastor

2 - 4% came because they had special needs

1 - 2 % came because of crusades

75 - 90% came because they were invited and brought by friends, relatives - neighbor and colleagues.

Thus we can safely conclude that worshipers come through the influence of people who are friendly, who gave sense of belonging, and make them feel part of the family.

COMPARING SECULAR WITH CHURCH SITUATION.

Inference from business research findings on why

customers stop patronizing businesses show the following.

A research survey of why customers quit found the following:

1. 3 % move away

2. 5% develop other friendship

3. 9% leave for competitive reasons

4. 14% are dissatisfied with the product

5. 68% quit because of an attitude of indifference towards the customers by the owner, manager or some employees.

A typical business hears from only 4% of its dissatisfied customers. The 96% just quietly go away and 91 % will never come back.

WHY WORSHIPPERS STOP COMING

Is it not true that if all the visitors that ever visited our churches stayed, we would have grown several times our present size? Why they move away and never come back may have much to do with First time impression.

While 3% may have stopped coming to church because they moved away from the environment, 5% develop friendship in other fellowships, 9% of worshipers probably stopped coming due to the distance and other inconveniences they encountered in coming to the church. 14% move away because their needs are not met. 68% most likely stopped coming because of indifference towards the worshipers by the Pastor. officials or members of the church. Indifference starts from the front door of the church to the pulpit. The worshipper simply walks out through the back door. 91 % never come back!

Ushers, Protocols and Greeters hold one of the keys to the back door of any church. They may not be the reason why people come to a church for the first time, but they are one of the reasons for first timers' second time return.

Chapter 14: What To Do When The Worshipper/Visitor Calls, Is Angry, Defensive or Confused

The nature of the church office front officer puts him/her in a position whereby he comes in contact on weekly basis with numerous worshipers. For him to be able to fulfill his role effectively as a frontline worker, he must be able to analyse and understand the various personalities of worshiper he comes in contact with.

Apart from being very polite and tactful in the ways he deals with them, specific skills are required for the specific personalities. Below are some tips to handle some problems that front-line officers face weekly.

TO AN AGGRESSIVE WORSHIPPER:

* Maybe a worshipper that is argumentative, obstinate, rude, prejudiced etc.

* Always wanting to dominate by attacking you ceaselessly no matter how helpful you prove.

YOU MUST:

* Not over react at his aggression.

* Find any reason for his action and try to let him say his mind but stay your ground. Do not apologetic, but sound helpful.

* Don't win the battle and lose the war.

TO AN EXPERT (KNOW ALL) WORSHIPPER:

* May want to feel important, over confident, very cautious

* Very knowledgeable, very Spiritual

YOU MUST:

* Make him feel important

* Seek his opinion about RELEVANT issues to the subject

* Be tactful and exhibit your knowledge of whatever the subject is

* Need a little more time to convince him

* Don't win the battle and lose the war

TO AN IGNORANT WORSHIPPER:

* Educate him on the subject. Direct him to the proper officer in charge, if necessary

TO AN INDECISIVE WORSHIPPER

* Maybe very hesitant (cannot make up his mind perhaps because of misconception)

YOU MUST:

* Not give him too many options (eliminate most of the unnecessary ones)

* Show him I to 2 closely knitted options

* You might have to decide for him

* Your knowledge of the subject and the worshiper behaviour may help you greatly.

TO A QUIET OR SILENT WORSHIPPER:

* It may be his nature to be quiet or embarrassed somehow or may be shy and so cannot talk properly.

YOU MUST:

* Not do all the talking, allow him do some and talk at his own pace (softly, gently) to enable him to understand you.

* Stay away from pointed questions that may embarrass him.

* Ask open-ended questions

* Not ask question that require mono-syllable answer (Yes or No)

* Not put much pressure on him

* Make him feel the decision is all his

TO A COMPLAINING WORSHIPPER:

* Always finding fault with whatever you do or say in the church

* May be nervous, usually worried because his mind is over active.

YOU MUST:

* Be sympathetic and always offer support for his problems. If possible, re-assure him, but be brief

* Do not get defensive

* Do not take his criticisms personally

TO AN AGREEABLE WORSHIPPER:

* Might want you to like him

YOU MUST:

* Be tactful and polite, but do not shift ground

* If possible, offer some advice on the subject

* This type of worshiper seems easy to handle, but

tactfulness is very important

TO AN EMOTIONAL WORSHIPER:

* May breakdown suddenly shedding tears or otherwise
* They are very sentimental

YOU MUST:

* Convince him, no matter the circumstances, but be tactful

However, the particular situation of the, worshiper determines what styles the frontline use in handling them. Generally, politeness, tactfulness and sounding helpful all the time are very important.

Chapter 15: Twelve (12) Deadly Sins Of Frontline Church Workers (Ushers, Protocols, Counsellors, ETC)

1. Talkativeness and gossiping on duty - among themselves during service, Sunday School or with members, revealing secrets.

2. Grumbling/ murmuring.

3. Not submitting fully to leaders (Rom. 13: 1 - 5)

4. Pride (Prov. 6: 6 - 19) - Because they are easily seen by everyone - they become popular and pompous

5. Over-familiarity with spiritual matters - Because they have the privilege of opening eyes during prayers, they see everything going on. They take record of souls saved, backsliders, response to word of knowledge etc. and caring people under power. They don't know when God is moving or not or talking to them as individuals.

6. Expecting rewards or praise from Leaders or Pastors (Rev. 2:2; 1 Cor. 15: 58).

7. Inferiority complex, feeling ashamed of oneself because of inadequacies, grammar, age or background

(II Tim. 2:15).

8. Respect of Persons - James 2: 1-4, 9

9. Taking advantage of position, preying on rich members, new converts, new comers, weak people or opposite sex for marriage. (An Usher was proposing to a lady under anointing in a conference).

10. Disunity among Ushers - 1 Cor. 12: 12, 17 - I9.

11. Overlooking personal, spiritual growth - SS. 1:6;1 Kings 20;39 - 40;

    Is. 56: 6.: 7

12. AWOL (Away Without Leave) - II Thess. 3:6

Chapter 16: Eight More Things Not To Do As An Usher/Protocol/Greeters

1. Do not stand in the door way. Standing in the door way is blocking the entrance. When you stand just beside the door way, you offer visual welcome and greeting.

2. Do not indulge in discussion with worshippers at the entrance of the hall of worship. If you need to make an enquiry or felicitate with a worshipper you know, make it very brief.

3. Do not reach out to shake hands, especially the opposite gender or an older person, unless the worshipper first extends a hand to you. Remember, a hearty hand shake from an usher may be a painful experience for some worshippers.

4. Do not touch a worshipper on the shoulder, elbow or back. In other words, don't let your hand shake extend beyound the elbow. If worshippers extend such gesture to you; accept such as gesture of friendship and nothing more!

5. Do not engage in small chat and discussion with another Usher when the worship service is on.

6. Avoid attracting attention of worshippers to yourself by the sound of your shoes.

7. Do not wear anything that draws attention to yourself. Dressing must be smart and appropriate for the occasion and moderate in all respect. Take your cue about what dress is appropriate from the congregation in the absence of standard uniform.

8. Do not comment on the appearance of the worshippers and first timer. Let them feel free to worship God as they come. Leave apparel direction to the pulpit and appropriate leaders.

Chapter 17: How To Make Ordinary Become Extra-ordinary

A brother was about finishing from Sunday School's Workers in Training class in a Gospel Church. When it was time to ask the students to indicate the area of their giftedness and callings, the brother realized he did not have the aptitude to teach - he was not even well educated. He could not sing well, as he didn't have a good voice. He looked within himself as to what God would use. He found out he had strong physique, a smiling face and interest in people, with a lot of endurance. He settled for the work of an usher in the church - but a different type of usher. He found his way to the camp for 3 days prayers and fasting - with one major topic "God make me a special usher". He added an oath: "If you make me one, I will always spend every weekend in prayers and fasting for this job."

He resumed work on Sunday directing people, shaking hands and smiling. It was soon noticed that most of the response for altar call, either for salvation, healings, dedication or answer to the call unto the ministry was coming from a particular section of the church auditorium. Not only that, most times after service, the people from this particular section were always most fervent during prayer times, and they seem to spend longer times than others praying after service in their seats. Things went on. The pastorate took note and decided to investigate. The people that do this do not do it for show. They may not sit there following week. Only those sitting there respond that way. Our Usher brother was invited for explanation. It was then that the secret came out. His was not an ordinary usher.

His secrets were:

1. He saw the need for God's help because of the importance he attached to his ministry as an usher

2. He was consistent with God

3. He took care of his own personality - he realized that he was the first that worshipers meet before the service and after the service.

section D
PERSONAL GROOMING FOR PUBLIC

MINISTRY

Chapter 18: You Never Get A Second Chance To Make A Good First Impression

It is amazing that only few workers and relatively fewer ministers have really been trained or taught in the basic grooming habits. Several Christians may regard this aspect .of their ministry as been too simplistic or carnal. This is very essential to include in our present discussion.

Have you nat tried to embrace a colleague and the body odour puts you off? Or you try to lean over to whisper a word and the bad breath was so nauseating you never tried to be close. Brilliant minds, highly gifted with tremendous anointing, but nobody ever takes the time to tell them the essence of personal grooming.

PERSONAL APPEARANCE

The great man of God, Arch Bishop Idahasa, once said, "you are addressed as you are dressed". The way we dress must reflect Whom we are representing.

"So Pharaoh sent for Joseph, and he was quickly brought, from the dungeon. When he had shaved and changed his clothes, he came before pharaoh" (Gen. 41:41). Since Joseph required the approval, and acceptance of Pharaoh and those of Egyptians, he shaved his beards, because the Egyptians were not favourably disposed towards beards. He changed his clothes - he

adapted to the environment.

We need to appear neatly dressed before God and our congregation at all times. 70 - 90% of your body is covered with cloth. People see what we are before they hear what we say. *"Also I desire that women should adorn themselves modestly and appropriately and sensibly in seemly apparel, not with elaborate hair arrangement or gold or pearls or expensive clothing"* (1 Tim. 2:9 - Amplified).

Remember you never get a second chance to make a first impression.

THIRTEEN PERSONAL UP KEEPS

1. At least one or two bath or shower every day

2. Brush your teeth after every meal use a mouth wash or simply brush teeth, first thing on waking up, last thing before going to bed.

3. Wash your hair at least, every other day or weekend.

4. Use a good deodorant daily (especially if you notice bad odour - you can't rarely smell yourself any way).

5. Keep your finger nails clean. I never knew the importance of manicure or pedicure early in my life. I didn't even know the meaning (Do you?). I only concluded it was worldly and for very carnal people. However the dictionary defines Manicure - as care of

the hands and finger nails, to cut clean and polish the finger nails (not necessarily to paint - but to polish). Pedicure - treatment of the feet, especially toe nails, corns (hardened skin on the toe) or bunion (inflamed swelling, especially an the large joint of the big toe).

6. Keep your shoes shined at all times. Most women feel they can tell quite about a man through the up keep of his shoes.

7. Check the back of your head, comb it properly before you set out-check it all the time

8. Shave everyday or whenever necessary.

9. Keep your shocks fresh

10. Take daily care of your underwear - singlet's etc.

11. If you have breath problem, take peppermint or hack with you - and exercise your faith till it disappears.

12. Keep your hair well grooms.

13. Get your rest - fatigue has taken more dreams, than the devil does. *"Come aside by yourselves to a deserted place and rest a while for they were coming and going and they did not even have time to eat"* (Mark 6:31).

Chapter 19: Ten Ways To Develop A Winning Personality

WHAT IS PERSONALITY?

Personality is the sum total of an individual, mental, spiritual and physical traits and habits that distinguish him from all others

It is the factor that more than anything else determines whether one is liked or disliked by his fellowman. It is the secret that makes men to be pleased with you. II Sam. 3:36; I Chrn 12:22.

1. SEEK TO CARRY THE PRESENCE OF GOD WITH YOU ALWAYS (I Sam. 3:19-21)

What do we need to do to carry the presence of God? Grow in your spiritual life, prayer life, bible studies, fasting, maturity, Discipline.

Results of spiritual growth include:

a. The Lord will be with you anywhere you go, you carry God with you, Your appearance anywhere will create a difference.

b. None of your words will fall to the ground. When you say "it is well" it shall be well, "God bless you", "God will do it". He backs you up.

c. All people around and beyond will know that you were established to be in that ministry. *"knew Samuel was confirmed as a Prophet of the LORD"* (NAS).

d. The Lord will appear in your assembly

e. He will reveal Himself to you continually.

2. TREAT OTHERS AS YOU WOULD WANT TO BE TREATED

Mat 7:12. Think of how the other person feels, not how you are feeling. An average person likes to be regarded.

3. GIVE RECOGNITION TO PEOPLE

As soon as you see a worshipper/member, politely acknowledge his/her presence. Never, never, never ignore a worshipper. Acknowledge each of them. Approval, praise, love are the greatest motivations of life. Is he/she dressing fine? Tell him/her. Is he/she punctual? Is he/she a good singer? Are the children well behaved or neat? Be generous with kind statement.

4. START EACH DAY WITH A CHECK UP

"Study to show yourself approved unto God a workman that needs not to be ashamed" (In II Tim 2:15). It is only God that looks first at the inward part, man looks first at the outward. First impression will be based largely on your appearance and those of the place of worship. Take care of anything a worshipper sees, feel, smells or hears. Make list of things that need to be checked before the start of each service, to make sure the worshipper gets a good first impression.

a. Start with yourself: are you clear eyed well groomed, well shaven, well dressed, hair well fixed and free of bad breadth or body odours?

b. Is the place of service clean and orderly?

c. Is every Usher, Protocol and Greeter physically and mentally prepared to give every worshipper a first class performance? Take a little extra time at the start of each day to look at the business through your worshippers' eye.

5. CULTIVATE LISTENING ABILITY

We need to cultivate the habit of listening to what people are telling us, instead of concentrating on what we are going to say and miss a lot of the message. We should learn to listen with three ears.

- Listen to what people are saying

- Listen for what they are saying

- Listen for what people would like to say but can't put into words

6. DEVELOP TACTFULNESS

You are tactful when you do and say the right thing at the right time. Tactfulness is a way of relating to others without being rude or becoming an embarrassment or threatening to someone else's sensitivity

7. BE FLEXIBLE

Flexibility does not mean compromise on truth. It only means being able to shift ground when necessary, in order to fit changing circumstances. Flexibility of personality enables you to understand and sympathize with another's point of view.

As usher should avoid situations that will require use of harsh word, physical force, argument or misunderstanding. It is better to loose an argument with a worshipper and win his commitment to the church and Christ, than win over an argument, but chase him from the church or Christ.

8. DRESS APPROPRIATELY

How you dress can also have a significant impact on how others perceive you. The best dressed person usually is the one whose clothes and accessories are so well chosen that the individual does not attract undue attention. Neatness makes your dressing adequate. Notice the style of your clothes also in relation to your congregation. Examine the condition of your hair, condition of your shoes and nails. Looking your best is only the secret of being your best.

9. ALWAYS BE PUNCTUAL

Time is your most precious tool. It is one of practical virtues of an attractive personality. When you are late you cannot be at your best. It is even an offence. Calculate the number of minutes you were late with the number of people in your congregation and see the effect. An usher who gets late for 10 minutes in a church of 1000 members has wasted a total of 139 days of the people's time

10. SMILE AND SMILE ALWAYS

The man with attractive personality and disarming smile knows how to make a first and lasting impression.

Chapter 20: Seven Ways To Develop Positive Mental Attitude In Ministry

1. FEEL GOOD ABOUT YOURSELF

"As a man thinks in his heart so he is" (Pro. 23:7a). Improve your appearance and be neat. Stop running yourself down. There is a lot that is right in you.

2. CHANGE YOUR ATTITUDE ABOUT OTHERS

Give yourself a chance before judging others. To be happy at work, change your attitude about others. Stop wasting your mental energy on analyzing past events, start thinking about what to do now (Matt. 7: 12.)

3. DECIDE ON A GOAL AND PUT A TIME TABLE ON IT

Take small steps. Don't set targets that will disappoint you.

4. FEEL, ACT AND THINK ENTHUSIASTICALLY

5. KEEP COMPANY OF OPTIMIST

Avoid the company of losers. Distance yourself from habitual grumblers and the kind of people who only talk negatively (Pro. 13:20).

6. STOP BEING MOODY

A mood is a feeling of depression and a negative attitude. Switch to positive thoughts and your feeling will change. A merry heart has continual feast (Pro. 15:13, 15) and does good like medicine (Pro. 17:22).

7. EXERCISE EVERYDAY – WORK UP A SWEAT

Physical exercise always goes a long way towards making you feel good and alive. It is a healthy way of living.

Chapter 21: Cultivating Poise And Right Self Image In Front Office Relations

"But the end of all things is at hand: be ye therefore sober, and watch unto prayer. [8]And above all things have fervent charity among yourselves: for charity shall cover the multitude of sins. [9]Use hospitality one to another without grudging. [10]As every man hath received the gift, even so minister the same one to another, as good stewards of the manifold grace of God. [11]If any man speak, let him speak as the oracles of God; if any man minister, let him do it as of the ability which God giveth: that God in all things may be glorified through Jesus Christ, to whom be praise and dominion for ever and ever. Amen." (1 Peter 4:7-11).

"And whatsoever ye do in word or deed, do all in the name of the Lord Jesus, giving thanks to God and the Father by him" (Col. 3:17).

DEFINITIONS:

POISE: Graceful and balanced control of bodily position or movement. Quiet, dignified self-confidence and self control.

SELF IMAGE: The way you see yourself (impression you have about yourself).

Front Office Management is basically about people/customer relations but we shall attempt to relate this to the way we receive and relate to visitors and new comers in our midst. Our focus in this section include carriage, language, presentation, dressing, PR, friendliness, attraction.

A) CARRIAGE:

Most of us judge people based on how they look and talk, especially if we're meeting them for the first time, though this is not right. What this implies for us as ushers, greeters, protocol officers, counselors etc in the Church, is that the first impressions we give to visitors to the church are crucial in creating the right image. We therefore need to make good impressions when meeting people for the first time. The following tips will help us to look more confident:

*   Hold your head up when walking or standing

*   Look people in the eye

*   Stand straight with your shoulders back

*   Dress appropriately and be clean and neat. What you wear does not have to be expensive and should certainly not be loud.

*   Sit with your feet on the floor, legs together (especially for ladies) and back straight.

B) LANGUAGE (Col. 4:6):

Language is all about communication and starts with words. Before you start using a word, ask yourself, "Is this word saying what I want it to say or is it saying something different?"

Apart from the words, the way we say them also counts your body language should agree with the actual words. Words like "please" "thank you" and "sorry" should be used generously in our speech.

*   Do not be a bore. Do not dwell too long on what you

are saying. Well said is soon said.

* If your do not know what to say when meeting new people, take the focus off yourself and put the focus on the other person by asking questions about them that are not nosy. For example "Is this your new car?" is a nice question but "Oh you have a new car, how much did it cost?" is a nosy question?

* Do not explain yourself too much. It's a joy to converse with people who make appropriate comments and then stop talking.

* Talk in a strong but not loud voice

* Listen to the other person

* Know how to take hints.

C) PRESENTATION AND DRESSING (1 Peter 3:3 - 4):

We should try to dress appropriately for occasions, but most importantly we should be moderate. Remember that how we choose to drape (dress) the outer person is of little significance compared to our fundamental inner mentality. However, as front office managers in the church, our dress sense should be impeccable and formal.

D) PUBLIC RELATIONS AND FRIENDLINESS

"He who wants friends must be a friend! We should learn to show simple courtesies to people (1 Peter 3:8b) and reach out to them in genuine love and warmth, thereby making friends (1 Peter 3 : 8a). The golden rule "do unto others as you would have them do unto you" is of much relevance here.

Section E
WORSHIPPERS/HUMAN RELATIONSHIP SKILLS FOR USHERS, PROTOCOLS AND GREETERS

Chapter 22: Sound Human Relationship Skills For Ushers, Protocols And Greeters

"Therefore all things whatsoever you would that men should do to you, do ye even so to them: for this is the law and the prophets" (Matt. 7:12).

The above Bible text is not only the golden rule; it is the only rule in human relationship.

SIX (6) CHECKLISTS OF WORSHIPPERS' EXPECTATION

Develop a checklist of what worshippers will expect on getting to the church, apart from message and music. Your list must include:

1. Smiling and accommodating people

2. Safety and security of cars, persons and personal belongings

3. Comfort - clean seats, clean environment, private and hygienic toilets

4. Social convenience - not to be exposed, especially if coming late

5. A place worth inviting others to

6. Understanding officials - in case of having to make demands

CHURCH PUBLIC RELATION DUTIES OF USHERS

1. God's public relation officers: representing God and the church to every new visitor

2. He warmly welcomes visitors and worshippers with an outstretched and hand and smile to ease their tension and curiosity, and making them feel secure and at home

3. Seats them in comfortable accessible seats

4. Distributes bulletin, offering/tithe envelopes and all necessary information with them and supports the announcement

5. Making the visitor's day by reinforcing the good package of the service

THE TEN COMMANDMENTS OF WORSHIPPER/PUBLIC RELATIONS

1. The worshipper is the most important person in any ministry treat them as such

2. The worshipper is not dependent on us-we are dependent on them

3. The worshipper is not an interruption to our ministry, but the reason for it

4. The worshipper does us a favour when he calls - we are not doing him any favour

5. The worshipper is not there to argue with or match wits with - we are there to accommodate them

6. The worshipper is the person who brings his seeds - it is our job to fulfil those needs

7. The worshipper is part of our ministry - not an outsider

8. The worshipper is deserving of the most attentive treatment we can give - so give it

9. The worshipper is the person who God uses to finance our ministry

10. The worshipper is the life blood of any fellowship - without them we have no ministry

Chapter 23: Ten Ways To Be A Great Host

A good host makes a difference, whether you are visiting a home or a church. What does it take to be a great host and welcome guests in a manner that will increase their desire to return?

Here are ten ways to be a great host

1. Invite your guests with a personal invitation: You must draw up a list and send out invitations.

2. Provide Good and Tasty meals: A good meal of the word of God is what makes people come. Every Sunday, visitors to your church come expecting to hear good messages. Pastors should spend more time praying and studying to cook good meals and feed good meals to the people.

3. Arrive early to make sure everything is ready for the guests' arrival: Planning is required. Welcoming guests does not happen accidentally.

4. Ensure your environment is neat and attractive: You only get one chance to make a lasting impression, good and neat environment is critical. Whatever is touchable or seeable should be checked for quality. A church should invest more in what people see and use more often. By communicating touches of quality, the people attending the service will know that excellence is recognized.

5. Greet the guests warmly at the entrance and escort them to their seats: Determine in advance, where people will seat and escort them there. Your protocol unit should be prepared.

6. Assist guests in understanding what is taking place: Don't let them feel like outsiders. Explain service schedule and items that may seem strange to them.

7. Anticipate and answer questions as much as possible in advance, so guest do not have to ask questions like: Where the restroom is located, children nursery, exit doors, service schedules. Help guests to fit in. Help them get over your religious jargons, songs and service format.

8. Ask questions as if you were a guest visiting your church and answer them: If you were a guest visiting your church.

   a) Would you be impressed with the facility and landscaping?

   b) Would you be able to find the restrooms without asking?

   c) Would you feel comfortable leaving your child in the nursery

   d) Would you understand what takes place during the worship services?

   e) Were you embarrassed or pressured during your visit?

   f) Would you be greeted and accepted as you are?

   g) Would you come back next week?

9. Do something special extra to make guests visit special.

10. Walk guests to the door and invite them back.

Chapter 24: Fifteen (15) Rules Of Human Relations

We need to bear in mind some simple rules about interacting with people:

1. Say "hello" to people you know (it shows you are glad to see them. silence means " you are there, but so what?")

* Greet people by name - it shows you care and makes2.people feel good. If you have trouble remembering names, practise saying them when they are fresh in your mind e.g if you are meeting someone for the first time, say they names several times as you converse with him.

3. If your are greeting an adult, stand up.

4 Look people in the eye, it shows interest, honesty and friendliness.

5. Shake hands where possible (stand up to do this) and always offer the right hand, even if you're left handed.

6. If you find yourself with people who don't know each other, introduce them.

7. Address the older person first e.g. Pastor Charles, please meet my friend, Tunde. Tunde, Pastor Charles ministers in my church.

8. Address a woman before a man e.g. Sister Arin, meet my colleague, Segun. Segun, Sister Arin is my Pastor's wife.

9.*Be all things to all people. When you see someone in need, lend a hand and you will be surprised when you are in need, many hands will be there to support you.

10.Have a cheerful disposition towards people.

11.Grace should season all we do. True grace should begin in our hearts and flow out through our actions.

12. Praise what is proper, but note that excessive praise does not have value. Do good to others, a little at a time but often.

13. Do not expect people to always handle you with care, like glass.

14. Become a versatile person and come out of your shell.

A person of many excellent qualities equals the worth of many people. Impart the full scope of your enjoyment of life to your cycle of friends and followers, and there by enrich their lives.

Chapter 25: Maximize "Moments of Truth" With Your Guests

Thinking of a church in terms of moments of truth creates a powerful tool to help us address and evaluate the quality of our friendliness. If enables us to redirect our thinking from programs to serving those Christ has called us to reach.

WHAT IS "MOMENT OF TRUTH" (MOT)?

A moment of truth is any occasion in which a person comes into contact with and forms an impression of your church. The end result of any contact is either positive or negative about your entire church.

WHAT HAPPENS EACH TIME A GUEST ENCOUNTERS THESE "MOMENTS OF TRUTH" AT YOUR CHURCH?

The most important moments of truth for a guest are their first and last ones. The total perception comes into play, but the first and the last moments of truth are extremely powerful.

TEN MOST IMPORTANT MOMENTS OF TRUTH

1) WHEN THEY RECEIVE AN INVITATION TO YOUR CHURCH:

This invite may come through a personal invitation, bulk SMS, direct mail, email etc.

2) DRIVING BY YOUR CHURCH BUILDING:

If your church is located in a high traffic area, you can be certain that many people are driving by each day. While they drive up to the facility, another moment of truth is added to their previous encounter. They will notice if the exterior walls and windows of the building are attractive. If there are parking spaces clearly marked for guests. The landscaping and general cleanliness of the church environment.

3) WALKING TO THE FRONT DOOR:

As people walk up to your church, a lot of thoughts race through their minds. What will they find inside the church building? Will they be well received? Are they appropriately dressed? Surveys reveal that 75 percent of people say they are more anxious the first time they enter a new place, such as a business, church or office than at most other times in their lives. 80 percent of adults visitors don't like to be treated specially or differently during service.

4) WHEN THEY ENTER THE FRONT DOOR:

The anxiety of new comers on entering the front door causes them to form most of their impressions about a church within 30 seconds of their entry. The following help a new comer to make up his mind either to return or not. Such things as: sound, smells, signs, pictures, bulleting, boards, colors, lightning and the general decor.

5) INITIAL CONTACTS WITH PEOPLE:

Are church members outgoing and approachable? Do they express an attitude of acceptance? Is there an honest friendliness? Are friendly people available to answer questions, give assistance etc. What is the general body language of people they meet? Condescending? Arrogant?

6) HOW ARE THE AMENITIES. SERVICES AND MINISTRIES?:

The experience of your guests will vary according to the ministries, amenities and services they need per time. Those with small children will be interested in the cleanliness, brightness and safety of the children church. Those that need the restroom hope to find it clean and odour free.

7) ENTERING THE SANCTUARY:

Guests entering the church auditorium look forward to meet smiling ushers and friendly people to graciously welcome them to their seats.

8) BEING INVOLVED IN THE WORSHIP SERVICE:

Guests hope to find an order of service that is not strange or complicated. They hope to hear familiar songs or new songs easy to learn. They look forward to feeling at ease and relaxed and hope the service will not go for too long. 70 percent would like that information about the church be made available.

9) ON THEIR WAY OUT:

Guests hope to be greeted by friendly people after the worship service, but not besieged. 78 percent of adult guests would like to be greeted individually after the service by people.

10) BEING CONTACTED DURING THE WEEK:

70 percent of guests like the idea of receiving a thank you note, e-mail, text message from the pastor during the week of their visit. 72 percent of adult visitors don't like the idea of your bringing gifts to their homes as thank you gift for visiting your church. They feel trapped.

Section F
MODERN TRENDS AND CONCEPTS IN

CHURCH SECURITY

Chapter 26: Safety And Security Awareness For Ushers And Security Officers

"Unless the Lord builds the house, its builders labour in vain. Unless the Lord watches over the city, the watchmen stand guard in vain" (Ps. 127:1).

SAFETY is usually defined as "being safe, freedom from danger" and Security is the "protection against loss and damage to persons and properties", which also means freedom from danger i.e. safety.

WHAT CAN CAUSE LOSS OR DAMAGE TO WORSHIPPERS AND CHURCH PROPERTY?

Of course, persons (worshippers) fire, accidents explosions and demonic attack. Hence, to ensure that persons, fire explosion or accidents do not cause loss or damage to worshippers, ministers or church property, the Church usher has to:

1. Pray, pray and pray

2. Keep watch (Jesus said, "Watch and Pray" - Mark 13

:33)

3. Patrol Round the Premises

4. Prevent Accident

5. Render First Aid, both Spiritual and Physical

6. Do other duties for the purpose of ensuring safety of persons or property.

We shall discuss these duties briefly.

PRAYER COVER

Ushers are modern day watchman set up by God to watch over the household of God (Ezek. 3: 17). The weapon they have is to live a strong prayerful life for continuos victory. They owe the church the responsibility to provide prayer cover. *"Except the LORD watches over the city the watchmen (Ushers) stand guard in vain"* (Ps 127: 1)

We are fighting against principalities and powers (Eph. 6: 12). The Usher is to pray in the spirit on all occasion with all kinds of prayers and requests. With this in mind, (the Usher is to) be alert and always keep on praying for all the saints (Eph. 6: 18 NIV). This prayer warfare is to be engaged in before coming to the church, individually, aside from once in a week/month corporate Night Vigil.

The Usher, like every other Christian, is commanded to pray without ceasing and continually (I Thes. 1:7). He is to pray in the Spirit all through the service, under his breath.

KEEPING WATCH

From the entrance to the car park, auditorium, offices and toilets and corners of the Church, the Usher keeps watch to ensure that no undesirable persons gain access to the church. This calls for a lot of discernment tact, fast thinking and discretion.

Several people are smartly dressed in the service but with devilish intentions. One of these entered our church, he was a white man posing as Managing Director of a group of companies. As it turned out, he came to defraud God's people.

A "gentleman" walked in another time and introduced himself as a Lawyer who just moved in from Port Harcourt, Southern, Nigeria. His wife was in the hospital, in a coma, after giving birth to twins. Now he needed money to buy blood for blood transfusion for the wife. He took the money from our church and disappeared into thin air.

One young man was discovered to be fumbling with another worshipper's bag during session of prayers.

A bomb was found in the auditorium of Yoido Central Gospel Church, pastored by Dr. Younggi Cho. It was the watchful eyes of the Ushers that discovered the bomb, evacuated the building, and sent for Bomb Detonating Experts.

Part of Watchfulness is to quickly pick up on going rumours, gossip in the church etc. Investigate, analyse and inform the authorities.

He watches for destructive tendencies of some individuals especially children.

A watchful usher will search round the premises, first thing before the service commences and will be patient to conduct a final round check at the end of every service - not only for items left behind, but for individuals, either lingering behind or sleeping in a corner. A young man was forgotten after a church service on a Friday. The sanctuary was not opened until Sunday. He had gone to a corner during the Friday Prayer meeting to take a short nap, which extended beyond service time.

Watchfulness also includes, preventing children from straying during service to the streets.

SECURITY PATROLS AND BEATS

It is likely that most patrolling will be done during service, especially in the evening service. The route and starting point of your patrols will be changed frequently to ensure the element of surprise in coming across offences against Church rules and deliberate acts of damage and theft. Changes to routes and starting points should not be made within anyone's motive. Periods of 24 hours routes should cross upon themselves. You will find however that patrols are arranged so that you will visit fire and other hazard areas at definite intervals, and this is one requirement that you should fulfil conscientiously. Effective communication with your Usher/Security Office (if it is manned) or Gatehouse, or other Usher/Security staff is vital - you may need to call on their services at a moment's notice, or they may need to pass information or instructions to you.

Your Patrol Record is also a vital document not merely to record times and incidents, but to ensure that action is taken at the earliest, to remove and remedy victims to safety. As you will see, ushering/ patrolling is one of the most important functions of Security and calls for vigilance and astuteness as well as a clear understanding of what constitutes a fire or safety hazard.

It is often said that a good Usher/Security Officer has a good 'nose for trouble'. As a Usher/ Patrolman, you will need to use all your senses - an eye for the unusual situation, your hearing to detect suspicious sounds, and your nose to smell smoke, gas leaks, or other hazardous materials.

Here are some of the most common situations you may come across:

1. The outbreak of fire caused by acts of carelessness, electrical failures, overheating of equipments, sparking among flammable materials, etc.

2. Premises left unlocked or excess lighting left on.   .

3. Machinery and other equipment left running overnight that should have been shut down.

4. Slippery floor caused by oil spills in the generator area.

5. Windows left open or broken that would make things easy for intruders.

6. Maintenance or other church officers breaking safety rules:

7. Flooding or leaks of water from equipment, sprinkler systems, damaged roofs etc.

This list is by no means exhaustive and to it can be added many hazards particular to your Church. Get to know where special hazards could exist in your premises, and make sure that you check them thoroughly, and report immediately any unusual occurrence.

FIRE PATROLLING

During patrol, an usher is to inspect every part of the Church premises as soon as possible after every service, and systematically at intervals with special attention to danger points.

1. Switch off any electrical appliances mistakably left

on: Air conditioner, Electric fans and lights.

2. Investigate any smell or burning

3. Extinguish naked flames

4. Move anything that can easily bum from sources of heat

5. Stop immediately any leakage of oil diesel or inflammable liquids from generator hose, vehicles and any other source.

6. Glance at waste paper baskets in offices and at corners to ensure that no smothering fire has been ignited.

7. Check that all firefighting equipment is present, serviceable and unobstructed.

ACCIDENT PREVENTION

To ensure that premises are safe, the Usher should during his patrols watch for unsafe conditions such as:

a. Patches of oil or grease on roads or footways

b. Cavities or protruding slabs in footways, broken tiles or holes in tilted floors.

c. Broken or defective hand rails on stair case.

d. Dangerous packing of vehicles.

e. Dangerous or reckless driving of vehicles

f Horseplay by children especially in dangerous areas e.g. Generator house or Engine Control Room.

g. Interference with electric services and switch gear - especially those without good knowledge.

h. Excessive accumulation of refuse in passages or walking areas.

ESSENTIAL PRECAUTIONS TO TAKE

a. Never use water on electrical fire or oil fire.

b. Never attack fire from a point where the fire is between you and your means of escape.

c. Call fire service immediately.

d. Be familiar with the use of fire extinguishers and use at the early stage of any fire.

e. Note that the British standard for painting extinguishers for quick recognition are:

   i. RED Signifies Water/Extinguisher used for free burning or solid materials such as woods, paper, clothes, plastics, rubber etc.

ii. CREAM for foam Extinguisher. For flamable liquids such as kerosine, petrols, spirits etc.

iii. BLUE for dry Powder Extinguisher: For fire involving flammable gasses e. g. Cooking gas, acetylene, natural gasses, hydrogen.

iv. BLACK for Carbodioxide Extinguisher for fire involving combustible metals such as Sodium, reactive zinc, phosphorous etc.

v. GREEN for BCF Extinguisher. For fires involving electricity.

Chapter 27: Twenty Security Red Points Of Danger In The Church

A. SUNDAY WORSHIP HAZARDS

1. Seating postures of ladies in micro miniskirts facing the altar.

2. Members/worshippers who want to settle score/grievance with the pastor or the church. A pastor was kidnapped for 3 days in the midst of a major programme. One was almost stabbed by area boys at the instance of aggrieved members of the church.

3. Mentally/spiritually deranged persons in services. A pastor was slapped during service as he was preaching and attempting to emphasize his point in front of his audience.

4. Vindictive acts of worshippers against worshippers. A praise worship leader was stabbed during worship session by a fellow choir member (who was under

suspension). She fell down in the pool of her own blood and was rushed out of service.

5. Car theft from church car park. A car registration number was called out during services asking the owner was to come and repark as another car owner wanted to move out. As the person got there and about to repark, the waiting man opened the door, shoved him to the passenger side and drove him off in the car. A case of kidnap and car theft on Sunday morning.

6. Assassination during service. A note was received from car park that the owner of a car was needed urgently by her far. On getting to her car, she was shot at close range and she dropped dead, while the assassin escaped in a waiting car.

7. Children straying and wandering across the street.

   - Cases of accident involving children

   - An eleven (11) years old boy was led by an adult posing as friend of the boy's father for some moments before the boy gained consciousness and revolted.

8. An usher was found using broom stick with chewing gum to pilfer money from offering box. Another was caught filling the boot of his car with offering from services.

9. Worshippers left behind after service. Someone went to sleep in a corner during prayer meeting on a Friday. Services closed and doors locked. He was there till Sunday morning.

10. A time bomb was planted in the church of Dr. Yonggi Cho.

11. A Pastor was kidnapped on his way from crusade stand.

B. CHURCH PREMISES HAZARD

1. Exposed electrical wires, fittings and broken sockets

2. Slippery floor with water or oily substance

3. Premises left unlocked, windows left open.

4. Excess lighting left on.

5. People loitering in the church premises either during or after services

6. Cars left over night. Police traced three stolen cars to a church premises. The cars have been parked in the church for 3 days.

7. Unidentified parcels

8. Unauthorized access to the premises. A prayer hall was opened on Monday morning; 16 cigarettes stubs were found littering the prayer carpet.

9. Unprotected stair - case or balcony with no railings. 30 children recently fell off from a weak railing along

a stair case as they tried to avoid being beaten by their teacher. Broken skulls and fractured bones and torn flesh were the result. A stitch in time definitely would have saved everything.

TEN HELPFUL SECURITY TIPS IN THE CHURCH

1. Pray for guidance and protection. *"Except the Lord build the house, they labour in vain that build it; except the Lord keep the city, the watchmen waketh but in vain."* (Ps. 127:1).

2. Beware of vagrants that come to the church looking for salvation only long enough to get some money so they can replenish their drug supply. Even decent men play on the church intelligence.

3. Be discreet with vital information on the church members' tithe and giving record. Access to this should be restricted to key, tested church functionaries. A group of armed robbers went from house to house in a neighborhood with a list of rich prominent members - they call out the names and

identify them as church members before disposing them of their belongings.

4. Develop water tight system of removing offerings from the sanctuary and counting the money.

   (a) Once carried, don't allow the box to be let down for a second until it reaches the counting tables.

   (b) Have a minimum of two appointed counters in the room at one time. Money often disappears at this point.

   (c) Keep tight security around this area.

   (d) Keep information tight as to who holds what amount of money.

   A vicar of a church who happened to be the secretary of the diocese was with N100,000 ($700) meant for organizing diocese pastors conference. Three men drove towards the counseling room. Two stayed with security at the gate, while one strolled in and demanded for the money with the vicar. The robber went in straight to the particular spot where the money was kept and removed it and locked up the vicar and his family in the toilet. The robber and his colleagues exchanged pleasantries with the security men at the gate and drove out.

5. Be on the look out for people who may want to settle domestic or personal matters in the church.

   (a)   Some unbelieving husbands come to beat their wives in the church.

   (b) Monitor People on suspension

6. Develop security awareness mentality in the church.

   - Car park visitors. Notes during services. Why was the windows opened? Who entered last?

   - Constantly patrol premises - sniff out all corners.

7. Get familiar with local law enforcement agents in your area. Civil defence, corps, police etc. Make use of the expertise within your congregation. Ask uniformed men in your church questions and for security advice.

8. Protect your minister: Front row facing the altar, only decent dressing should be allowed. No one to come to altar unauthorized.

9. Be alert during time of crises, spiritual conflict in your community and special meeting with well-known minister.

10. Open your eyes, ears, nostrils, heart and mind. In other words, be alert to your surroundings and immediate environment and report to relevant authorities.

CRIME WATCH - TUESDAY, DECEMBER 29, 2009

Gunmen Invade Church, Kidnap Julius Berger GM

Sola Adebayo, Warri

The General Manager of the German construction giant, Julius Berger Plc, in Warri, Delta State, Mr. Francis German, was on Sunday abducted by four gunmen.

The unnamed German was abducted during the Sunday service at the Redeemed Christian Church of God, located at Delta Steel Company Roundabout,

Aladja, Udu Local Government Area of the state.

The armed kidnappers invaded the church at 9.25am and seized the top official of the leading construction company to an unknown destination.

His whereabouts could be ascertained on Monday as family and police sources said the suspected kidnappers had not contacted them.

Our correspondent gathered that trouble started for German, who is also the director of PEE BODY Hotel, Aladja, when he was invited out of the church to repark his navy blue Mercedes Benz E-Class 350 car. It was said to be obstructing the free flow of cars in the church premises.

Four armed youths emerged as the German was repositioning the car and pushed him to the passenger's seat. One of the youths drove the car from the scene in company with the German and his colleagues.

But on Sunday evening, the police intercepted the vehicle at Patani, about 80 kilometres away, being driven by one of the suspected kidnappers. The Police Public Relations Officer, Delta State Command, Mr. Charles Muoka, confirmed the report, adding that the suspect was being interrogated. Muoka expressed conviction that the German would be released unhurt and advised members of his family not to pay a ransom to secure his freedom.

Chapter 28: Basic Investigation And Intelligence Network In The Church Setting

A criminal investigator is the person who collects facts to accomplish three fold aims: to identify, locate the guilty party and to provide evidence of his guilt. The tools of the investigator are, for the sake of simplicity, referred to as the three "Is" in varying proportions to gather the facts which are necessary to establish the guilt of an accused in a criminal offence or trial. The tools are information, interrogation and instrumentation.

THE TOOLS FOR INVESTIGATION

(1) INFORMATION:

This is the knowledge about the crime which the investigator gathers from other persons. There are basically two types of information:

a. The information from regular sources as conscientious and public spirited citizens, church records and the files of other agencies.

b. This is got from cultivated sources as from planted

informants, cab drivers licensed owners and employees in general. Information is by far the most important since it answers the question "who did it". By the marvellous expedient of simply questioning a knowledgeable, and often anonymous individual, the identity of the perpetrator of the crime, and usually his motive are revealed. The investigation at once acquires direction, and subsequent steps are meaningful rather than merely experimental.

(2) INTERROGATION:

This includes the skilled questioning of witnesses and suspects. The success of information depends on the intelligent selection of informative sources. The effectiveness of interrogation varies with the craft, logic, and psychological insight with which the investigator questions a person who is in possession of information, by questioning is the most prized talent of the investigator. Usually the novice investigator often over-looks the most obvious approach of asking the suspect if he committed the offence. Instead, investigators tend to be carried away by their eagerness to use the more refined techniques of modem crime detection. The guilty person is in possession of most of the information required necessary for a disciplinary action, and, if he is questioned intelligently, he can usually be induced to talk. A confession which includes details that could not be known by an innocent party is the most convincing form of proof. An investigator should look upon a suspect or reluctant witness as a person who will yield the desired information, if he is questioned with sufficient skill and patience.

(3) INSTRUMENTATION:

This is the third method and it includes the application of the instruments and methods of physical science to the detection of crime. **This instrumentation includes fingerprint and foot-print system, modus operandi files, communication system, surveillance equipment such as telephoto lens and detective dyes, searching apparatus such as the X-ray unit and the metal detector and other within the scope.** A thorough training in the resources of instrumentation is of great importance to an investigator.

THE INITIAL INVESTIGTION FOR AN INVESTIGATOR

Commit the matter to God's hand and ask for insight. *"Call unto me, and I will answer thee, and shew thee great and mighty things, which thou knowest not"* (Jer. 33:3).

a. Before the scene is disturbed, the investigator must have been trained to look patiently for clues at the scene and now deduce what materials are likely to furnish useful information.

b. An investigator should not form a pre-conceived theory on the way to the scene of crime.

c. Visit the scene immediately. Delay may entail the destruction or loss of witness.

d. Assess, at the scene, the truthfulness or otherwise of the complaint.

e. Study the scene carefully. Stop, look and think.

f. Seek for exhibits. Label and make note of the exact they are found. Look for the modus operandi (the method of operation) of the criminal and make an accurate record of the scene through sketch plans and photographs.

g. Be scientific and be finger-print conscious.

h. Be methodical, do not hurry.

I. Do not waste time recording full statements from witnesses at the scene. Get their story, make notes and record their names and addresses.

j. Make local enquiries.

k. When you record witness statements, make a thorough job of it.

l. Study your case carefully and constantly.

m. Admit your mistakes and correct them.

n. Seek advice and guidance whenever necessary.

o. Documents relevant to the case should be filled at the back of the case-file.

p. The diary of action must be full, accurate and up-to-date.

q. At the end of the investigation, the summary of all the material evidence will be prepared together with the brief and accurate report stating the title, the full facts of the case in correct sequence and recommendation based on the facts.

Chapter 29: Observation And Perception Intelligence Training

Square face

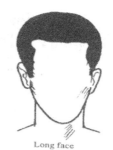

Long face

Broad face

Long Head

High Crown head

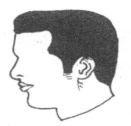

Flat in the Back

Chapter 30: Medical Emergencies

Take any person in the midst of a medical emergency (heart attack, stroke, seizure, onset of child birth, exhaustion fainting or any peculiar symptom) to a private room. Talk to the person on how he feels and what he thinks the problem is. Relay his answer to health care professionals when they arrive.

HEART ATTACK

Usual complain is usually that of squeezing chest pain, sweating, weakness, nausea or a feeling of "impending doom". WHAT TO DO let the person sit or lie down. Loosen any restrictive clothing and assure the patient. If the person's heart stops, administer mouth resuscitation.

SEIZURES

Seizures are caused by high fever, infections, brain injury, stroke, epilepsy and demonic oppression. Call for professional help, don't be alarmed. Gently, lay the person on the floor on his side. In case he vomits or salivates, loosen restrictive clothing around the neck and chest and place a bitestick or pieces of leather between the person' teeth, if there is the danger of biting his tongue, hold the arms and legs tight enough to prevent injury.

BLEEDING

Apply pressure directly over the wound with a clean cloth or your hand. Try to raise injured part above the level of heart, whenever possible.

BREATHING DIFFICULTIES

Open the victims airways and hit the head at the back. If an adult stops breathing, pinch the nostrils and cover the mouth with your own. Begin with four rapid breath, then use one breath every three seconds. If an infant stops breathing cover both nose and mouth with your mouth. Use four quick breathing and one breath every 3 seconds.

BROKEN BONES

Never move the victim because you may hurt the broken bone. Apply a splint carefully, if help is delayed.

BURNS

Relieve the pain of minor burns with cold water and prevent from contamination.

CHILD BIRTH

Assist a woman with labour pains to a private place. Encourage her husband to stay with her and calm her. Keep relaxed and then call medical personnel.

DIABETICS

If they fail to take their insulin, they may suffer from seizure, nausea or other serious side effects. Let insulin be taken with normal food intake. Without a normal meal, insulin may take blood sugar too low.

Section G
LEADING A VIBRANT HELP MINISTRY

Chapter 31: Challenges And Responsibilities Of The Head Ushers, Protocols And Greeters

The head usher/protocol work corresponds closely to the duties of Deacons in the first century. I Tim. 3:8-13 is a useful model for us as Head Ushers/Protocols.

In like manner the Deacons (must be) worthy of respect not shifty and double talkers but sincere in what they say, nc;t 'given to much wine, not greedy for base gain (craving wealth and retorting, as ignoble and dishonest methods of getting it).

They must possess the mystic secret of the faith (christian truth as hidden from ungodly men) with a clear conscience and let them also be tried and investigated and proved first; then (if they turn out to be) above reproach, let them serve (as deacons) (the) women likewise must be worthy of respect and serious, not gossips, but temperate and self controlled, (thoroughly) trustworthy in all things.

Let deacons be the husbands of but one wife, and let them manage their: children and their own household well. For those who perform well as deacons acquire a good standing for themselves and also gain much confidence and freedom and boldness in the faith which is (founded on and centres) Christ Jesus. (Amplified)

AVOID OVERWORKING YOUR PEOPLE.

Adopt a rotation system - If an usher/protocol has to work one service, he is able to sit with his family and hear God's word during the 2nd service. People who are already busy in the church but wants to usher can be used for special meetings or as a substitute for absentees.

BUDGETING AND INVENTORY

Your organizational skills have an impact on how efficiently your department runs. Work out an appropriate budget with the finance committee/Treasurer that allows you to purchase the necessities used in your department. Umbrella dnd raincoat to assist people in the parking lot or rainy days. Walkie talkie, torchlight, batteries, candles, matches, e.t.c.

Always keep inventory of your supplies like offering envelopes, pencils and other needed items. You should workout a system that allows you to submit a requisition order to the church at least two weeks in advance.

Have an area in the church that is the ushers corner/office. Keep it neat and organized so each usher knows where to locate things.

Chapter 32: Establish Thirteen Guidelines And Procedures For Your Operation

1. **Attendance** - Head counting: When, How, Where

2. **Children** - Monitoring

3. **Emergencies** - Medical, weather, Fire

4. **Offering** - Recovery and Counting

5. **Sermon activities** - What to do before, during and after sermon

6. **Absenteeism Notice** - If unable to usher, length of notice

7. **Confidentiality of information and details concerning church members** - The church council,

office or title and contribution kept private

8. **Dress Code** - Neatly pressed suit and ties, sandals not acceptable - Make ups and distracting hair not acceptable.

9. **Health** - Do not usher if you are nol well

10. **Incident** - Reports. Please report in writing if you are hurt on the premises or an accident whereby another person is hurt.

11. **Sign-in** - Please sign in and out for an accurate record

12. **Training** - Orientation procedures for new ushers get them familiar with church building layout and several week working beside an experienced usher.

13. **Termination** - When an usher becomes counter-productive, the head usher arranges a discussion session. If violation continues, dismissal occurs.

We recommend that you write down your policy and distribute to all ushers.

SIX WAYS TO RUN YOUR DEPARTMENTAL MEETINGS PRODUCTIVELY

1. Keep your Pastor informed on the time and place of your organizational meetings. Encouraging his attendance and input at your meetings or on occasional basis will be a great morale builder for your workers. You will also know what is expected of you.

2. Encourage your workers' input during your meetings. Write down areas of improvement as well as areas of complaint.

3. Keep a record of your meetings and attained goals to give your group a sense of accomplishment.

4. Try problem solving as a group and listen to each person's concerns.

5. Encourage the ushers to share success stories of how effective one of the ushering methods has been. An usher may have a testimony on how his live and friendliness towards a reserved person finally brought them around.

6. Send your meeting minutes to your Pastor to keep him informed of any changes and gain his approval for new policies you are preparing.

GUEST SPEAKER RECEPTION

During special meetings be on hand to receive the guest speaker and take him to your senior pastor. Confirm from the pastor before arrival, if he has to be lodged in an hotel, where? Provide. an escort - either your deputy or 'yourself to accompany him to the place of residence. Confirm his needs. Confirm the hotel before his arrival. Ensure it is neat and ready and comfortable. Leave copies of programmes with him.

BE FEARLESS

God has called you. You can't die in battle. *"The righteous are as bold as a lion"* (Prov. 28: 1).

Chapter 33: Seven (7) Ways Of Counting People During Service

I first came across this concept from my voracious reading of Dr. Dag Mills' excellent books on 'Church Growth and Shepherding'.

TYPE 1 COUNTING

'Type 1 Counting' is the counting of the number of human beings physically present at a particular meeting. It is the headcount of people in attendance. This is the headcount. I believe this type of counting is the most informative of all the types of counting. However, it is probably the least used way of counting because it is usually the lowest!

The fact is that only a fraction of your members come to church on Sundays. If you use the Type 1 Counting, you are only talking about a fraction of the real number of people that God has given you to look after. In spite of this, I still prefer to work with Type 1 Counting because it provokes me to work harder.

TYPE 2 COUNTING

This is the total number of people on the church register. Many churches quote this Type 2 number as their membership. The Type 2 counting is larger or smaller depending on how far back the church will go in counting its registered members. The figure also depends on whether the church updates or revises its membership lists frequently. It also depends on how a church revises the membership list. Some churches have what we call "active members". For some couple, an active member is someone who attends a service at least once a month. For others it is someone who attends every Sunday service. I consider an active member to be someone who comes to church during the week, Le., not only on Sundays. For others it is someone who belongs to a smaller cell group.

All of these can vary the eventual outcome of the Type 2 Counting. What this means is that my ten thousand figure may be different from your ten thousand figure.

Some pastors give a Type 2 figure as their regular attendance. When you attend your church and see the actual number of people, you may be very disappointed. There is often a sharp contrast between the number of people physically present and the number of people the pastor claims to be his members. You may even think the pastor has a problem with lying or exaggeration. We have seen situations where the Type 1 Counting is as low as ten percent of what they claim to be their membership. The church may claim to have ten thousand members, but only one or two thousand are present in the service.

TYPE 3 COUNTING

This type of counting is often used during conventions and crusades that run over a few days. It is the cumulative count. The total number of people who attend the meetings is counted. For instance, they could say that the convention was very successful and that, ten thousand people were in attendance. What they actually mean is that two thousand people came each night for five days! This type of counting is often misleading, as it does not give an accurate picture of the truth.

TYPE 4 COUNTING

This is where the seating capacity of the building is used to estimate membership. Sometimes a building has a maximum capacity of three thousand. During a programme, the pastor could say there were three thousand people in church. This is because the whole church looked full, so the assumption was that three thousand people were there. This is a wrong assumption. A Type 1 Counting could have easily revealed that only two thousand people were present. A hall, that is capable of seating three thousand people, can "look" full when only two thousand people are present.

TYPE 5 COUNTING

This is when pastors give rough estimates. They try to give a reasonable assessment off the crowd. The pastor thinks he can assess the numbers present in the crowd. He makes estimates based on experience. He concludes for instance that there are about three hundred people present. Sometimes these rough estimations are quite accurate but at other times they can be totally misleading.

The pastor of the local church is likely to give a higher Type 5 Counting than the pastor of a sister church who is visiting and observing. The local pastor would say, "There are about two thousand people present." The visiting minister would say," I think there are about one thousand two hundred people present." The visiting minister would not like his rival's church to look too big, so his figure would therefore be much more modest.

TYPE 6 COUNTING

Type 6 counting is what I call 'wild and unreasonable

guessing'. Some years ago when we had about eight hundred people attending our church, I met someone in London who told me," I heard you had a convention and there were seven thousand people present."

I asked him, "Who told you that?" He gave the name of the woman who had said that. She had said, "I was in the meeting myself and there were about seven thousand people present." I always wondered, "How did she get the figure 'seven thousand'?" She must have had a shot at Type 6 Counting - wild guessing!

TYPE 7 COUNTING

This type of counting aims at outdoing everyone else. A pastor mentions a figure that is higher than any other figure being mentioned in town. If the largest church is said to be around five thousand, he will always have around six or seven thousand members. This pastor is suffering from the spirit of lying and exaggeration.

Chapter 34: Fourteen Significant Numbers Every Church Needs To Count

There are some important figures that every pastor must always be constantly aware of. Each of these figures has some significance. Each meeting has its special role to play in the life and development of the church.

This section is adapted from the writings of Dr. Dag Mills and experiences of veteran pastor.

1. THE NUMBER OF PEOPLE PHYSICALLY PRESENT ON SUNDAY MORNINGS (TYPE 1 COUNTING OF SUNDAY SERVICE)

This number is only a percentage of your true membership. In a normal church, a large number of people are absent on some Sundays. This why the number can fluctuate so much. The Sunday service attendance is the best number to use for monitoring progress in a general way.

2. THE NUMBER OF PEOPLE PRESENT AT A WEEKLY SERVICE

This tells you the numbers of the very committed members you have. Most serious Christians make time to attend church during the week. You will find the anointing and flow of the Spirit is different on a weekday service. A corporate anointing manifests because of the gathering of faithful ones. Lukewarm and religious attendees do not dilute the atmosphere.

3. THE NUMBER OF PEOPLE PRESENT AT SMALL GROUP OR FELLOWSHIP MEETINGS

This number shows how developed the internal structure of the ministry is. There are some churches which can command thousands of people for a special convention; however they are not able to mobilize fifty people on a regular basis for small group meetings. It is important to have these small groups so that they can meet the needs of the members at a personal level.

4. THE NUMBER OF PEOPLE WHO ATTEND FASTING AND PRAYER SESSIONS

This tells you the number of spiritual soldiers you have. This is very different from the swelled up convention attendance. It should be the goal of every pastor to build up a large core of spiritual warriors. These people may be more dependable.

5. THE NUMBER OF PEOPLE AT A CONVENTION

The convention crowd contains many people who are moved by excitement. There are many "miracle seekers" and "sign watchers" in attendance.

6. THE NUMBER OF PEOPLE ABSENT AT EACH CHURCH SERVICE

This is a very important number. It tells you how many people are falling away. It is probably an indication of how hard the pastors and shepherds are working. Perhaps they are not being prayed for and they are not being visited.

7. THE NUMBER OF PEOPLE IN THE CHOIR OF THE CHURCH

The choir of the church is like the flower of a plant. It is often the part of the church that the outside world sees. It is often a reflection of the organizational skills of the church. It tells us how well the pastors are making use of the talents within the congregation.

8. THE NUMBER OF PEOPLE IN THE CITY WHERE YOUR CHURCH IS LOCATED

A church's size is always related to the size of the city in which it is situated. The largest churches in the world are found in the largest cities in the world. For example, if 0.1% of your city's 4 million population is in your church, then, your church population would have to be 4 thousand. If the membership shoots up to six thousand, you would still form only 0.15% of the population. This figure makes you relatively insignificant.

The figure must be determined every year for us to know how great an impact we are making in the city. If this percentage is insignificant, it must motivate us to have more visitations, more prayer, more fasting and more witnessing. It means that we must have more pastors, more shepherds, more churches, more ministries and more fellowships. We must invite more people, do more follow-up, have more crusades and release more power.

9. THE NUMBER OF PEOPLE WHO GIVE THEIR LIVES TO CHRIST EVERY SUNDAY

This tells you how conscious of lost souls the pastor is. It shows you whether members are inviting non-Christians to church. It tells us whether the church is fulfilling the Great Commission in getting people born again.

10. THE PERCENTAGE OF PEOPLE WHO ARE SAVED IN THE CHURCH

Occasionally, it is interesting to find out how many people got saved in the church. This tells you how original the church is. Some churches are made up of breakaway members of other churches. Since this was the source of the majority of their members, they often don't know how to win souls for themselves. Every church must know how to intentionally win souls and assimilate new converts.

11. THE NUMBER OF NEW CONVERTS WHO ARE STILL IN THE CHURCH AFTER TWO MONTHS

This tells you whether follow-up is being done.

12. THE NUMBER OF LAY WORKERS IN THE CHURCH

This shows you how involved the general congregation is in the ministry. It tells you what percentage of the church is asleep. When a human being is asleep, only eight percent of his body is at work. If only eight percent of your members are active, it means your church is asleep.

13. THE NUMBER OF PEOPLE WHO PAY TITHES

This is a reflection of the number of truly loyal people you have. The Bible says, *"For where your treasure is, there will your heart be also."* It tells you how many people in the crowd have their hearts solidly planted in the church.

14. THE NUMBER OF PEOPLE WHO ATTEND THE 31sT DECEMBER NIGHT SERVICE

Traditionally, this is a very well attended service. From my experience, it is the best attended service in the whole year. Superstitious people run to the church so that God will see them in Church as the New Year dawns. All of those you haven't seen throughout the year may finally show up on 31st December. The pastor is usually encouraged by the 31st December crowd. This swollen number usually regularizes within a few weeks.

Chapter 35: Record Keeping In The Help Ministry

"Be sure you know the condition of your flocks, give careful attention to your herds" (Pro. 27:23). One church bulletin said it all on record keeping it reads "We count because people count. The President and Exco of a Rotary Club approached me when I was Group Personnel/Training Manager of a group of companies in Ikeja, Lagos. They wanted to give the Employee Award to any deserving member of our organisation. Just one best employee in three organisations. We went into rewards. We finally came up with one fellow.

(1) A muslim

(2)　Married with 4 children

(3) Joined company ten years ago

(4)　Absent for one day in ten years because he lost his son

(5)　Was late for ten minutes in ten years

(6)　Never took sick leave in ten years for one day - He had catarrh and cough. An average time of resuming work 7am. Factory resumes 7.30am.

(7)　Always among the first to resume work because he clock in always before 7am. Among the last to clock out at 4:35 instead of 4.00pm he spends time to arrange his work for following day.

(8) No query, no warning, nor suspension, no disciplinary case to his name in 10 years.

Can you beat his record? Even our born again employees agreed he was the one worthy of the award. That was the essence of record keeping.

WHY KEEP RECORDS?

1. **IT HELPS TO KNOW THE CURRENT CONDITION OF OUR UNITS, MINISTRIES AND PEOPLE.**

   "Suppose one of you has a hundred sheep and loses one of them. Does he not leave the ninety-nine in the open country and go after the lost sheep until he finds it?" (Luke 15:4). How do you suppose he would have known one was missing if not for effective record keeping? A church administrator confides in me that their ushers count church attendance, every 30 minutes of the service. It helped them to know the fact that majority of their members arrive the service after praise and worship and other "preliminaries" to hear

only the word. So the pastor decided to put message first early enough in the service. This made service to be full on time.

2. IT HELPS TO FOCUS ON THE AREA THAT REQUIRES IMPROVEMENT AND ADJUSTMENTS.

3. RECORDS PROVIDE INFORMATION ON THE RATE OF PROGRESS OF THE UNIT AS IT AFFORDS COMPARISON WITH.

Where we are now and where we are coming from, as well as where we are going.

4. IT HELPS IN WISE PLANNING FOR FUTURE GROWTH AND DECISIONS

"Any enterprise is built by wise planning, becomes strong through common sense and profits wonderfully by keeping abreast of the facts" (Pro. 24:3-4 -LB). Units records help the ministries to plan. Ministry records help the church, the church helps the zone. The zone helps the district, district helps National Headquarter, National Headquarter helps International Headquarter.

5. **WE USE RECORDS FOR REASONABLE PROJECTIONS AND ESTIMATES IN LAUNCHING A NEW PROGRAMME AND GOSPEL WORK.**

   "Suppose one of you wants to .build a tower. Will he not first sit down and estimate the cost to see if he has enough money to complete it?" (Luke 14:28).

6. **IMPROPER RECORD LEADS TO CHAOS, CONFUSION, SHADY PRACTICES AND EMBARRASSMENT.**

   A bank manger helped to uncover a fraud that has been carried out in the church for five years. He became curious while going through the offering analysis of the church for 5 years and discovered that there was no $20 in the offerings on any Sunday or midweek. It was traced to the person that deposits the money and to the Pastor's secretary who always remove every 20 dollar bill in the offerings and bank the rest. By this time he has accumulated half a million dollars.

QUALITIES OF GOOD RECORDS

1. A good record must be easy to keep. Recording and maintaining the record should take the barest minimum of time.

2. A good record should fulfil a specific task.

3. It must be simple to understand. The record should be based on knowledge and procedures which are common to all or which could be explained to all easily.

4. It must provide enough details.

5. It must be versatile. It must serve more than one purpose. A record which serves two or more functions saves time and sometimes energy.

WHAT RECORDS TO KEEP

Register of services (blue, book register). Announcement book, Sunday school register and rewards, membership register.

Church workers register. Register of baptism, register of marriages, register of naming/dedication, register of funerals, tithe registers, fellowship registers, financial records and assets register. Offering register.

Statutory Records:

Will include: Constitution, Policies, Procedures, Records/minutes of meetings, Financial statement of Account, Certificate of incorporation, Deaths or lands and contracts with suppliers drawing and correspondence and letters.

Every unit of the Church needs to keep accurate records of minutes, resolutions, monthly/quarterly reports, documents comprehensive membership register as well as attendance records per meeting and new souls/converts. If any group in the church corresponds with another person or body outside the church, this corresponde.nce should be copied to the Pastor in charge e.g. national Head Ushers here just invited me as guest speaker for their training - I noticed that our general overseer was copied, why? The Pastor is ultimately responsible for all activities that take place wit~in and outside the church.

Sometimes these records are scattered around in the homes of church members, among old records or at the church head office.

The following records are essential in the church setting

1. Church service Record/Speaker, text attendance, souls saved, visitor's testimonies.

2. Church membership Records/ active, inactive; transfer, transition.

3. Staff Personnel Files

4. Sunday School Membership Records/Important information on students

5. Achievement Records

6. Training Records

7. Financial Records

Chapter 36: Seeing Your Church From The Eyes Of A Newcomer

The following is a possible checklist of items you would like the newcomer to observe and comment on in his or her feedback. Note that some of the items (i.e. nursery, youth department) may only be relevant if the newcomer is a person needing that sort of ministry.

FACILITIES

* Parking (ease, accessibility, signage)

* Ease in determining main entrance

* Landscaping

* Ease in finding the church

* Exterior signs (condition, clarity, size)

* Signage in finding where I need to go once inside

* Exterior of facility and church buildings (paint, curb appeal)

HOSPITALITY

* Greeting (by anyone, warmly/coolly/too gregarious)

* Offered help in finding location/classroom

* Appearance of greeters

* Visible name badges

* Offered bulletin/worship folder

* Knowledgeable of facility/class locations/church information

* Refreshment

* Did I feel comfortable as a newcomer, or under a spotlight?

NURSERY

* Signage/ directions

* Cleanliness

* Staff (adequate number, competence, appearance)

* Facility (size, appearance, equipment

* Check - in system

* Security

* Check - out system

* Pager system

CHILDREN

* Teacher there/semblance of order

* I met the teacher

* Child was greeted, made to feel at home

* Directions to classroom

* Introduction/orientation

* Equipment

* Decorations

* Take home materials

* Check - in system

* Check out system

* Follow - up

YOUTH

* Teacher there/semblance of order

* I met the teacher

* Youth was greeted, made to feel at home

* Directions to classroom

* Introduction / orientation

* Equipment

* Decorations

* Follow-up

WORSHIP SERVICE

* Arrival time

* Auditorium appearance

* Seating (availability, comfort)

* Help offered to find eat

* Could I see the screen?

* Could I follow the service items?

* Was the music balanced (vocal versus instruments)?

* Did the worship service flow freely?

MESSAGE/SERMON

* Lengthy

* Clarity

* Interest

* Relevance

* Notes

* Pastoral perceptions (attire, friendliness etc.)

* Content

* Audio (soft, loud, quality)

* Friendliness (general feel, warmth)

* Left understanding theme of the service?

* Length of service

* Relevance (contemporary, liturgical, traditional flavour)

* Did I feel informed about what I was to do/when?

REST ROOMS

* Signage/directions

* Lighting

* Decor

* Aroma

* Cleanliness

VISUAL IMAGE PACKAGE

* Bulletin/worship folder (printing, graphics, clarity, informative)

* Newsletter

* Brochures

* Business card

* Advertising

* Logo

* Signage

* Foyer area

* Information availability (arrangement, thoroughness, appeal)

FOLLOW - UP

* Appropriate amount (too much, too little)

* Type of follow-up received

* Overall comfort (embarrassed, felt welcome etc)

* Friendliness of people

* Friendliness of pastor/staff\

MISCELLANEOUS SURVEY POSSIBILITIES

* Called the church for information and was well received

* Requests were followed up by appropriate staff

* Received the information by mail in _____ days

* How is the church perceived in the community?

* What are our strengths, weaknesses?

* Is this is a place where you would want to return? Why or why not?

* Is this a place where you would invite your friends/neighbours to attend? Why or why not?

BIBLIOGRAPHY

1. AINA, Albert O.,**ATTRACTING RETAINING & ASSIMILATING MORE FIRST TIME GUESTS IN YOUR CHURCH**, Lagos 2013

2. PAIGE, Lanier C., **THE WORK OF THE GREETER**, USA 2010

3. DAG, Howard Mills, **PASTORAL MINISTRY**, Ghana 2007

4. BUDDY Bell, **USHERS HANDBOOK**, USA 1996

CLS Courses

We are pleased to present the following courses to you for your church growth and also for the training of your pastors, heads of ministries, unit leaders, committee chairmen, church workers and newly appointed church leaders.

Moreover, we have self-employment and business ownership programme packages for those desirous of firing their bosses and hiring themselves.

Christian Leadership Skills Inc. has conducted these courses in the last 12 years across the country to churches in over 85 denominations. The results have been immediate growth in these ministries. Our own Sunday worship attendance went up by 42% in two months, after one of the courses, Total Quality Services.

LEADERSHIP/WORKERS COURSES

1.   How To Make Sunday School More Interesting

2.   Total Quality Services (TQS)

3.   Ushers Performance Improvement Course

4.   How To Double Your House Fellowship Attendance

5.   Evangelism Strategies That Work Today

6.   Developing The Leader Within You.

7.   Effective Leadership Skills In The Ministry

PASTORS/MINISTERS-IN-SERVICE SEMINARS

1.   Breaking Growth Barriers (200, 400, 600, 1000)

2.   Maximizing Your Ministry Potentials

3.   Developing Financial Intelligence In The Ministry

4.   How To Lead Your Church To Peak Performance

5.   30 Ways To Increase Your Church Attendance

6.   How To Increase Giving In Your Church

7.   How To Turn Around Your Church Finances

SELF EMPLOYMENT/BUSINESS SEMINARS

1.   45 Business Ideas You can Do With Little or No Money

2.   How To Fire Your Boss And Hire Yourself

3.   How To Make Your First Million

4.   Developing Your Financial Intelligence

5.   17 Ways To Invest

6.   How To Keep Your Customers Coming Back

7.   How To Retire Happily

COURSE DURATION

Each of these courses require 5 hours to conduct (preferably on Saturdays 10am - 4pm or vigils) in your church premises or any venue as desired.

CONTACT

You can contact the CEO of Christian Leadership Skills Inc., Rev. A. O. Aina on 08023010696, 08023228828 or 01-4812124 or better still at the church he pastors at Saabo Foursquare Gospel Church, 21/23, Adebowale street, off Aina Street, Debo Bus-Stop, Saabo-Ojodu, Lagos on Tuesdays - Thursdays (4pm - 8pm), Sundays (1pm - 3pm).

Take advantage of these courses and bring explosion to your church in 60 days

BEST SELLING BOOKS, CDs & VCDs
BY ALBERT O. AINA

1. Discover Your Work Beyond Your Job

2. 10 Top Reasons Why People Fall In Their Careers

3. Breaking Financial Hardship

4. Developing Wealthy Mindset

5. Don't Eat Your Future

6. How To Plant Your Tree Of Wealth

7. How To Generate Sound Business Ideas

8. Covenant Buttons For Raising Capital

9. How To Convert Your Ability To Cash

10. Convert Your Potential To Cash

11. Mind Your Own Business

12. Moneywise Strategies

13. Saving Strategies of Millionaires

14. How To Do Business Without Money

15. Don't Eat Your Future

16. Impartation For Divine Protection

17. 10 Top Reasons Why People Fall In Their Careers

18. Breaking Financial Hardship

19. Developing Wealthy Mindset

20. Don't Eat Your Future

21. How To Plant Your Tree Of Wealth

22. Habits Of Church Growth Pastor

23. The Church That People Love To Go

For your copies or bulk purchase, call:

Albert O. Aina

CEO of Christian Leadership skills Inc.

Tel: 08023010696, 08023228828

Email: albertoaina@yahoo.com

Website: www.christianleadershipskills.org

or at Saabo Foursquare Gospel Church

21/23, Adebowale Street, Off Aina Street,

Debo Bus Stop, SaaboOjodu, Lagos.

(Tues. Thurs. 4pm8pm, Sun. 1pm 3pm).

THE AUTHOR: ALBERT O. AINA

A Pastor, Teacher, Trainer and Church Management Consultant with a divine mandate to raise effective leaders for the kingdom, empower business people and motivate the young generation for a life of purpose and achievement.

Management. He rose to become Group Personnel/Training Manager over a group of companies. He became Managing Director/CEO before he was 30. His organizations, Alaryn Management Center Limited and Christian Leadership Skills, Inc run Leadership Conferences, Personal Finance Seminars, Business Coaching Camps and Church Growth Conferences for thousands of Profit and NonProfit organizations. spanning close to two decades in the Foursquare Gospel Church. He is currently a District Overseer in the same organization. His wife is focused on singles, academic excellence and A chartered member of Institute of Personnel Management and Nigerian Institute of Rev. Aina and his wife, Lara are Senior Pastors of small, medium and mega churches. Rev. Aina is currently serving as National President, L.I.F.E. Theological Seminary

Alumni Association and serves on the Governing Council of the Seminary.

He is the President of AGAPE CONFERENCE INTERNATIONAL that has hosted teens, youths and couples from over 200 denominations since 1984. He has authored 35 motivational books to date.

Other books from the same author

1. Master Strategies For Church Growth And Multiplication

2. Follow-Up And Retaining Method's To Keep Your Church Growing

3. Breaking Church Growth And Financial Barriers

4. 100 Ways To Increase Church Finance

5. 101 Evangelistic Strategies That Grow Mega Churches

6. Healthy Systems For Healthy Church Growth

7. 101 Ways To Attract, Retain And Train Teens And Youths In Your Church

8. Dig Your Well Before You Get Thirsty

9. How To Manage Your Boss Before Firing Him

10. 21 Supernatural Tools For Business Success

11. Awake The Giant Within

12. How To Build Your Capacity For Future Relevance

13. Successful Church Financial Management

14. How To Create Multiple Streams Of Income

Made in United States
Orlando, FL
06 January 2025

56890271R00104